THE ORIGIN
OF THE SERIF

Demand for copies of *The Origin of the Serif* has been constant since Fr. Catich published it in 1968. The information found there is not available elsewhere, and Catich's theory on serif origins is not only original but persuasive. He connects it with a development of the Roman alphabet. Since the edition has been exhausted, Mary W. Gilroy the Curator of the Catich Gallery has prepared this new edition for publication.

The Catich Gallery was established in 1985 to commemorate the contribution of a great and original artist who taught at St. Ambrose from 1939 until his death in 1979. So far as is known, it is the only Gallery to concentrate on calligraphy, related arts and skills, and E. M. Catich work.

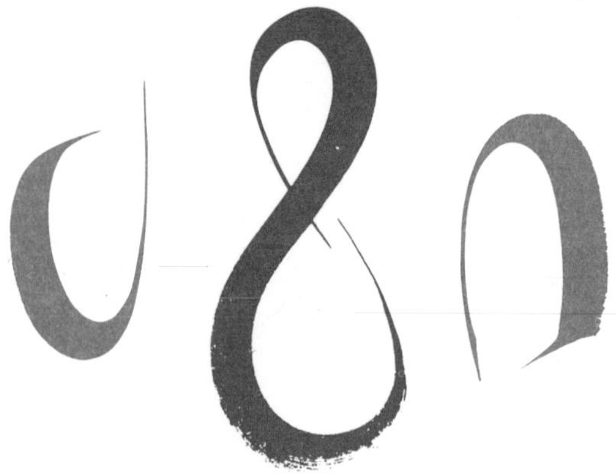

THE ORIGIN OF THE SERIF
▼
BRUSH WRITING &
ROMAN LETTERS

•

Edward M. Catich

•

Second Edition
Edited by:
Mary W. Gilroy

•

Catich Gallery
St. Ambrose University
Davenport, Iowa 52803

Library of Congress
Catalogue Card No.
91-072516

ISBN 0-9629740-0-5
ISBN 0-9629740-2-1 (pbk.)

First edition published in 1968.
Second edition 1991.
All Rights Reserved
Printed in the United States of America

Copyright by
Catich Gallery
St. Ambrose University
Davenport, Iowa 52803
•
1991

to

GRAHAM & NANCY CAREY

who love letters

Contents

THE ORIGIN OF THE SERIF

1

Introduction

This book, *The Origin of the Serif; Brush Writing and Roman Letters,* is the second of a trilogy. The first, *Letters Redrawn from the Trajan Inscription in Rome,* appeared in 1961. It dealt in detail with the history of modern information and misinformation on the Trajan Inscription, told why the chief source for knowledge of the Inscription is suspect, and gave full-size drawings of all the letters taken from the original inscription in Rome as these letters appear today.

The present book is the second of the series. It deals with the same problem — that of dispelling a strongly entrenched and highly respected set of errors—but approaches it from a technical rather than a historical point of view. It discusses the calligraphy and dynamics underlying the Roman inscription alphabet. It tries to show the primacy of writing over lettering and stone inscription making. It explains how misconceptions about stone lettering have influenced our thinking about letters and their origins. To achieve this, it concerns itself mainly with the instrumentality of the Roman writing, and with the least of all elements of letters themselves—the serif. The author hopes that the very smallness and apparent insignificance of the serif may act like the little edge of the wedge in splitting wide open the solid bulk of misinformation concerning our alphabet that has been growing since the days of the early Renaissance.

The third book of this series, if the author is granted time to complete it, is to be entitled "The Imperial Alphabet" and will consist in a thorough study of each of the Trajan letters not only from its visible, external shape but also from its equally important internal kinesthetic causes. From the knowledge of the internal factors it constructs those

3

letters, H, J, K, U, W, Y, Z, and &, which complete the alphabet but were not used in the Trajan Inscription. Since the Romans did not use the Arabic numerals familiar to us, the same method is used to shape numerals having an alphabetic kinship to the Trajan letters. To do this the author has tried to put himself into the position of the sign-writer who wrote the Trajan Inscription had that Roman been asked to write these missing letters and numerals.

2

Serif-origin difficulties

The origin of the serif in Roman inscription letters is one of the uncharted areas of paleography. We have no documentary information, for the Romans wrote no writing and lettering manuals. And we have few paleo-calligraphic artifacts to aid us. All we know about the serif, aside from its existence, is what has been written about it in recent times. Admittedly the serif is a minor part of a letter, certainly not an essential. It would seem, then, that one labors inordinately to write a book with the serif as a principal figure.

Practically all books on calligraphy resound with similar theories on the evolution of Roman letters, the determination of letter shapes, serif origin, and the primacy of the inscriptional alphabet. This familiar area of information has been traversed so often by student calligraphers and repeated so often in classrooms that it is accepted almost as fact. The aim of this book is not to repeat but to question this body of opinion. Yet any attempt to dissuade 'experts' away from this entrenched thinking about letters, serifs, etc., by the usual means, would undeniably be difficult. It is a truism that we convey new truths more convincingly when the message content is least familiar. In contrast, when the message travels along well-worn paths the writer runs the risk of boredom, or pre-judgment on the part of the reader. This is one reason of several why the serif, a small, non-essential appendage to letters, is used as an opening wedge into this complex and obscure area of paleography.

Over the years many aspects of Roman letters have had my attention and study, for example, how letters were made, what stroke sequences and directions were followed to fashion minuscules out of capitals, why we find open-lobed P's, splayed M's, long-tailed R's, pointed junctures in A, M, and N, internal angles on the curves of B and R, large, rounded internal junctures of stem and bottom arm only in B, D, E, and L, and other alphabetic facts. I finally realized that all these topics are intimately entwined with the problem of the serif, its purpose, and its origin, and that by explaining the serif one would in effect be explaining Latin letter shapes and the inscription alphabet.

Now the serif was a common item in ancient Rome. After the late Republic it appeared wherever the Romans went, in all classes of writing except informal, in all ages down to Rome's decline in the fifth century and, afterwards, in all western calligraphy. One is convinced that, like the letters it adorned, the serif was just taken for granted. No Roman bothered to tell us about it as no one bothered to tell us why Roman letters vary in widths, or why some strokes are thick, others thin.

For the serif to have been so widely diffused in Roman times and in so many varieties of existence over at least six centuries bespeaks a manner of production that was *natural and easy,* and as commonplace as making the curves, stems and arms of Latin inscription letters. And indeed, because it was so thoroughly commonplace and native to Latin letters, it would have been cause for wonder had any Roman explained it. Yet the theories advanced do not convince one that the serif was a natural, ordinary accessory to letters and easy to make.

One of the paradoxes of any new art expression is that, in the early stages of that art when solid creative thinking is going on, artist-workers are so concentrated on output that they have little leisure or desire to chart and explain their creative processes. It remains for a later age, the age of the critic, to undertake analysis and attempt reconstruction of that art's reasonableness. The process of criticism has taken place. It has been going on for the better part of a century. The serif has been catalogued and analysed in many ingenious ways. Yet suspicion gnaws, exposing tender spots in these explanations. It appears that more questions are formulated than are answered.

For example, how and why did the serif come to be and what purpose did it serve? Was it an effect of a preconceived pattern in the mind

6

of the letter-maker, or was it a by-product of the skillful use of his writing tool? Was it an esthetic refinement added by the worker, or a technical statement of the chisel working easily and naturally? Was it an imitation of reed-pen, stem finish or the vestigial remains of a scratched guideline? I believe that past answers to these questions have been inadequate.

In this inquiry conclusions are based on comparisons, on a knowledge of writing tools and their handling, reasoned conjecture, and an attempt to reconstruct the working conditions that prevailed when the serif came into existence. The chief proofs for a new theory are derived from an analysis of the inscription letter's inner nature, that is, by formulation of a provable basis for the internal kinesthetic dynamics proper to ancient inscription letters. But of all the re-assessed features of Roman letters none demolishes misconceptions of the Latin alphabet and inscription making so completely as does the serif. It is astonishing that such a small detail carries so much in its wake, as though the tail truly wagged the dog.

Definitions

In this book I propose to limit certain key words to the meanings I give here.

ESSENTIAL PART is that part necessary to a letter's makeup. Thus letter A has three essential parts, left oblique, bar, and right oblique.

Fig. 1. Three essential parts of letter A.

•

CONNECTIVE is the visible or invisible path made between essential parts of a letter by the writing tool.

Fig. 2. Connectives within letters.

LIGATURE is the visible joining between letters, or is a single character made up of several letters linked together.

Fig. 3. Ligatures.

•

STROKE is the visible mark made in one movement of the writing tool. A stroke can be 1) an essential part, 2) an essential part and connectives, or 3) several parts and their connectives.

Fig. 4. Various strokes.

•

TRACE is the path followed by the tool making letters. The trace may be partly visible as in carefully made letters, or wholly visible as in careless or quickly made letters.

Fig. 5. Traces of carefully made and hastily made letters HS.

9

PULL STROKES are the natural top-to-bottom and left-to-right strokes.

Fig. 6. Pull strokes.

•

PUSH STROKES are the opposed and rare right-to-left, and extremely rare bottom-to-top strokes. They are always combined with pulled strokes to begin and end letter parts. Push stroking demands a delicate touch and firm control, and is numbered among the advanced skills of the professional calligrapher.

Fig. 7. Push strokes combined with pull strokes. Push strokes are shown as full, and pull strokes as dotted lines.

•

The 'L' STROKE, consisting of stem and bottom arm made in one movement of the writing tool, is a characteristic stroke of letters B, D, and E.

10

LEBD

Fig. 8. The 'L' stroke of letters B, D, and E.

•

STROKE SEQUENCE & DIRECTION is the order in which essential parts are made and the direction these parts take. Thus there are 48 ways for making a three-stroke A (of which one way is correct) and 384 ways for making a four-stroke letter R (the correct way is shown in figure 9).

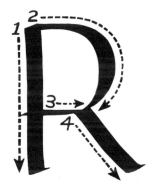

Fig. 9. The correct stroke sequence and direction for making R.

•

WRITING is the method of making letters in which each essential part of the letter is made in one stroke. In the diagram (Fig. 10) the letter is first written in four strokes, then in three, two and finally in one stroke, but each R is *written*. Whether or not the tool is lifted from the writing surface, between making the essential parts, the method used is *writing*. The kind of tool used does not affect the definition.

Thus one can write with stilus, pen, pencil, chalk, ball point, quill, brush, etc. The letters may be small as in everyday, informal writing with pen or pencil, or they may be six feet tall and written by the pro-

Fig. 10. Four written R's.

•

fessional sign writer using a ten-inch brush. But within its own genus, writing may be subdivided, according to accidental differences, into *formal, semi-formal* and *informal*.

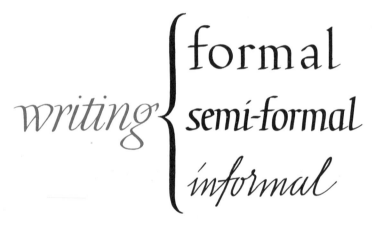

Fig. 11. Subdivisions of writing.

•

FORMAL writing is slowly and carefully made, without connectives or ligatures, upright, restrained, and intended for permanent use. The letters are separate from each other, and in general the shapes are designed in deference to the reading eye rather than to the writing hand.

12

Pentio ltíoh ndigle batem ayenl
kelo, Feefi Roleasco hvigreo Pfii

Fig. 12. Formal writing.

•

SEMI-FORMAL writing is written carefully but more quickly than
formal writing, and there is a tendency to slant the verticals, to compress
the letters laterally, to extend strokes above and below horizontal writing lines, and to show exuberance and freedom. Like formal writing it
is used by professional calligraphers and advanced amateurs. Semi-formal writing gives about equal consideration to the needs of the reading
eye and to those of the writing hand.

Aarempilon, Inoramtigrs

Fig. 13. Semi-formal writing.

•

INFORMAL writing is the everyday casual script of unprofes-
sional writers. The letters are not necessarily connected by ligatures.
It is not intended for permanent use and the demands of the hand are
satisfied rather than those of the eye. The usual tool for informal writing
is the pen, pencil, ball point, chalk, etc.

THIS INFORMAL

Fig. 14. Informal writing.

13

LETTERING is the method of making letters in which each essential part is made in more than one stroke. Thus a letter I made in more than one, letter L in more than two, or letter H in more than three

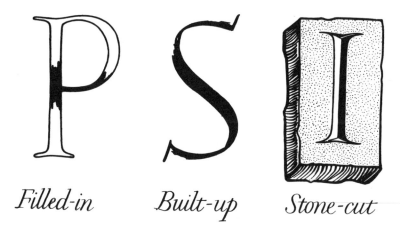

Filled-in   *Built-up*   *Stone-cut*

Fig. 15. Lettering.

strokes is said to be lettered. Varieties of lettering methods are gold leaf signs, inscriptions carved in wood or stone, and most advertising alphabets.

•

MAJUSCULE is the paleographer's name for a large or capital letter while MINUSCULE describes small or lower-case letters.

RVODSLITQPEFAE
omedtíolgrenudelt

Fig. 16. Majuscules and Minuscules.

14

CALLIGRAPHY is the art of making letters of fine quality by either writing or lettering and CACOGRAPHY is its opposite.

•

CANT is the angle between the thin edge of a square-ended pen, reed or brush, and the horizontal writing line.

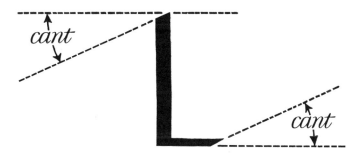

Fig. 17. Cant.

•

SERIF is the short cross stroke at the beginning and end of letter parts.

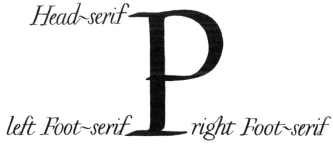

Fig. 18. Serifs.

•

STEM-WIDTH is the width of the vertical part of a letter, whereas BRUSH-, REED-, or PEN-WIDTH is the widest stroke made by each of these writing tools.

15

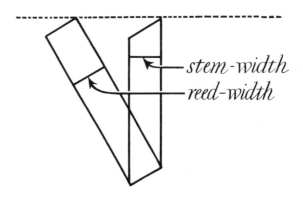

Fig. 19. Stem- and reed-width.

•

FILLET is the modulating curve between stem (or arm) and serif tip. The terms *crotchet* and *bracket* are often used for this letter part but are confusing inasmuch as the type character for enclosing printed matter has the same names.

Fig. 20. Fillets.

•

ARMS are the straight or curved horizontal parts of letters. BAR is the horizontal connector in A and H. Arms are found in letters B, C, D, E, F, G, J, L, P, R, S, T, and Z.

16

Fig. 21. Arms.

•

SHADED WRITING is the paleographer's term to describe writing made by the square-edged tool such as pen, quill, reed or brush. Sign writers call it THICK-AND-THIN, still others call it SQUARE-PEN or REED WRITING.

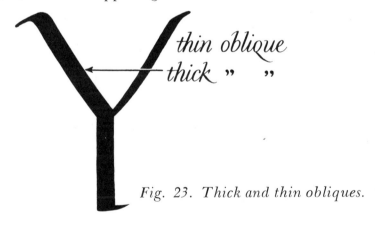

Fig. 22. Shaded or thick-and-thin writing.

•

THICK OBLIQUE strokes in letters A, K, M, N, V, W, X, and Y begin at the upper left and end at the lower right while THIN OBLIQUES course from upper right to lower left.

Fig. 23. Thick and thin obliques.

17

ANGULAR and ROUNDED JUNCTURES. In formal inscriptions letter-part junctures are angular except for some rounded junctures in letters B, D, E, L, and R. In figure 24 straight arrows point to angular and hooked arrows to rounded junctures.

Fig. 24. Angular and rounded junctures.

•

INTER-POINT is a word separator. The Romans did not space words, instead they used an inter-point, usually a triangle, between words.

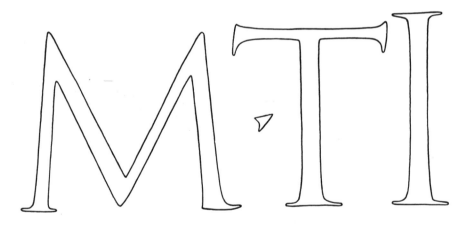

Fig. 25. Roman inter-point from a first century inscription now in the Vatican Lapidary Galleries.

18

V-CUT is the V-shaped trench made by the workman chiselling letter shapes in stones.

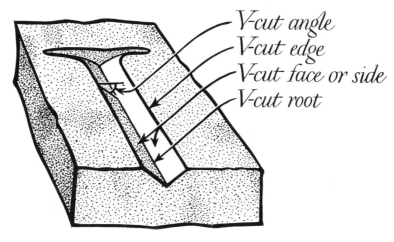

Fig. 26. The V-cut and its parts.

•

SHADOW, in V-cut letters, is the darkened portion of the V-cut caused by light from above and the side.

Fig. 27. Shadow in V-cut letters.

19

KINESTHESIS is a bodily sense, served by a special system of nerves, by which the patterns of muscle movements are controlled. It is the sense that guides gestures of all kinds from dancing to winding a watch. In writing it enables the hand to trace letters even when the eyes are shut. This sense is further described on page 140 sqq.

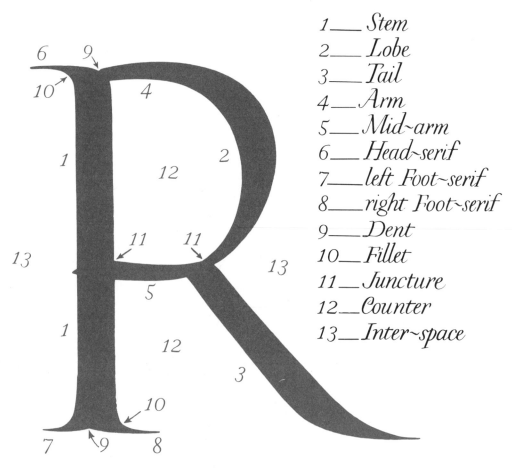

1 —— *Stem*
2 —— *Lobe*
3 —— *Tail*
4 —— *Arm*
5 —— *Mid-arm*
6 —— *Head-serif*
7 —— *left Foot-serif*
8 —— *right Foot-serif*
9 —— *Dent*
10 —— *Fillet*
11 —— *Juncture*
12 —— *Counter*
13 —— *Inter-space*

Fig. 28. Letter parts.

20

4

Trajan letters as evaluation

Roman capitals in the inscription at the base of the Column in Trajan's Forum in Rome are used in this book as an evaluating constant. This Trajan Inscription is generally considered the finest example of chisel-cut lettering of the best period of Roman inscription making. It was cut in 112-113 A.D. It also has the great merit of being well-known to typographers, paleographers and calligraphers. Almost every book on lettering acknowledges its superiority and most books show photographs of the Inscription's plaster replica in the Victoria and Albert Museum in London. A recent detailed treatment of this inscription including full size outline drawings of each letter (made from rubbings and squeezes of the original inscription in Rome), numeral mark, and punctuation point, as well as photographs, may be found in my earlier work, already mentioned, *The Trajan Inscription in Rome,* published by the Catfish Press, St. Ambrose College, Davenport, Iowa, 52803.

5

Present notions of serif origin

uthors who have speculated on the origin of the serif have given us a wide choice of theories. Most authors, referring to the stone-letterer's method of working, tell us that the cutter, about to carve a letter stem, first chisels a mark at the top and bottom of a letter stem to act as a "stop" indicator so that he will not chisel beyond the ends of the stems; and that, in time, these "stops" were the first letter parts to be chiselled, eventually becoming serifs. I list a few of these serif theories, advanced by their authors as established fact:

•

The manipulation of the chisel in stone caused the element known as the *serif* to come to be.

Oscar Ogg, *An Alphabet Source Book* (New York: Harper & Brothers, 1961), p. 35.

•

In the stone-cut capital the cutter felt the need of a neat square cut to end the stem of the letter. To define the free end, a sharp cut was made across it with the chisel, this cut extended beyond it on each side. Probably for the sake of uniformity, corresponding extensions were added to the thin strokes, and what was at first merely an attempt on the part of the craftsman toward neat workmanship later became an essential part of the letter itself. These endings are called "serifs" or "cornua."

Frederic W. Goudy, *The Capitals from the Trajan Column in Rome* (New York: Oxford University Press, 1936), p. 65.

•

In one detail . . . is the chisel's effect now evident, in what we call serifs . . .

Graily Hewitt. *Lettering* (Philadelphia: J. B. Lippincott Co., 1931), p. 36.

●

Aus der Meisseltechnick wurden die Serifen geboren . . .

Albert Kapr, *Deutsche Schriftkunst* (Dresden: Verlag der Kunst, 1959), p. 20.

●

Greater skill and the wish to produce a cleaner and more deliberate shape led almost inevitably to the finishing of chisel-made letters with some sort of wedge or serif shape. It is much more difficult to cut a neat sans than a neat Roman. The serif arises from the tool in this case.

Nicolete Gray, *Lettering on Buildings* (New York: Reinhold Publishing Corporation, 1960), p. 36.

●

As to the origin of the serif it may be assumed that they . . . were adopted by scribes for their ornamental value. Early Roman letters do not show a distinct serif treatment, Guide lines, however, drawn with a chisel to prevent overcutting (thus achieving letters of uniform height), were provided. Later we find serifs clearly defined and merged into the guide lines, distinctly becoming a part of the letter. As the esthetic value of the serifs, besides their practical use, became manifest, serifs were added on all free ends of straight lines.

Egon Weiss, *The Design of Lettering* (New York: Pencil Points Press, 1932), p. 14.

●

23

●

If the simple elementary form of the letter be cut firmly and directly, it will be found that the chisel will suggest how that form may be ornamented. This may be shown, for example, by an attempt to carve a quite simple incised letter with no Serifs and with all the strokes equally thick. In making the ends of the strokes there is a tendency to spread them into Serifs, and the letter is at once, in some sort, decorated.

A.E.R. Gill. Appendix B to Edw. Johnston's *Writing and Illuminating and Lettering* (New York: Pitman. 1948), p. 356.

●

The serif . . . followed the guide lines . . . scratched across the face of the stone.

Clarence P. Hornung, *Lettering from A to Z* (New York: W. Penn Publishing Corp., 1954), p. 10.

●

And because you cannot draw a V-shaped incision in stone to a square end that will define itself by its shadow, as a monumental letter

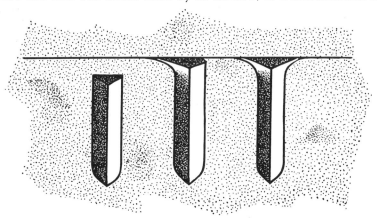

Fig. 29. Origin of the serif according to T. W. Stevens.

24

must do, classic craftsmen added the serif. This was at first a simple chisel cut across, following the scratched guide-lines, and defining the end of the stroke. But the serif soon came to be made of two minor incisions (see figure 29) and to have a certain proportion to the letter itself. Thus another lasting characteristic was added to Roman form.

Thomas Wood Stevens, *Lettering* (New York: The Prang Co., 1916), p. 27.

●

The serifs, or shoulders, were included to beautify and finish off the letter and to encourage the eye to pass along the line.

Russell Laker, *The Anatomy of Lettering* (London: The Studio Publication, 1959), p. 44.

●

Probably the major contribution of the chisel is the serif, the utility of which is immediately apparent when we incise a letter in stone. When the two cuts of an incised line are made, the finish is quite naturally weak. The simplest procedure is to come into the line at right angles; this relieves any tendency toward optical thinning of the vertical, and allows the finishing cut to be made more easily. Because they were utilitarian, these serifs became an integral part of letters, and were a beautiful adjunct.

Warren Chappell, *The Anatomy of Lettering* (Pelham, N. Y.: Bridgman, 1940), p. 1.

The serifs . . . were so important as a matter of cleaning up the stroke endings that they became a natural part of letter form.

Raymond A. Ballinger, *Lettering in Modern Use* (New York: Reinhold, 1952), p. 17. ●

25

et us examine the chief points of the ''chisel'' theory for the origin of the serif. The first objection is quite obvious. The implication is that the cutter does not have his chisel under control when cutting letter stems and therefore needs a ''stop'' mark to keep his chisel in bounds and thus to prevent over-cutting. But if the cutter does not have full control while cutting the letter-stem he would not have the ''stop'' strokes at the ends of the stem under control either.

It appears that a lack of knowledge of stone-cutting techniques is the reason for the ''chisel'' theory. From the questions they ask and the surprised interest they show when they first see letters being cut in stone, many calligraphers, I am convinced, confuse stone-cutting with wood-carving techniques. I am sure that most think that the stone letterer starts cutting from the outer edge of the letter, especially straight letter parts and stem ends. It is true that both stone and wood workers use mallets and chisels. But here the similarity ends, for chisel cutting in stone differs radically from carving in wood.

In wood carving the workman is always mindful of the wood's grain as he carves and slices. To prevent cuts made with the grain of the wood from splitting beyond the edge of the design the wood carver will first make limiting or ''stop'' cuts. In wood lettering, one usually makes these limiting cuts at the top and bottom of stems. Then too, the wood worker, using a knife instead of a chisel, will often cut each side of the V-cut at the outer edges of the letter stem to the root of the V-cut, not infrequently removing the V-cut, wood chip in one piece.

But in stone lettering there is practically no grain to contend with, certainly no sharply defined, predictable grain direction as in wood. In stone-cut lettering (except for very small letters, say, one-half inch tall) one starts from the center of the stem and, cutting along the stem and alternating from one to the other side, enlarges the V-cut to the letter's outer edge. One cannot chip away chunks of stone as one chips away large pieces of wood. The fact is that stone cutting is mostly a technique in which each mallet tap removes small, powdery particles of stone. Hence there is no need for stops at tops and bottoms of stems.

The objection to chisel-scratched, height-limiting guide lines as the origin of serifs is less obvious. Top and bottom guide lines for inscription layouts were made with a snap line covered with dry color or were chisel-scratched on the stone. In those inscriptions having them, the scratched lines will show up in a squeeze or on a very thin, tracing paper rubbing. These scratched lines were almost invisible and, unlike the letters, were not painted over, so they did not interfere with legibility.

The illustration in figure 30 shows a Pompeian inscription, now in the Museum of Naples, with a scratched head line. In this stone the

Fig. 30. Pompeian inscription with scratched guide line.

•

head line was scratched much deeper than the base line. The base line having weathered is hardly discernible. Figure 31 shows an inscription, now in the Vatican Museum with chisel-scratched head and base lines and figure 32 is a photograph of an early Christian epitaph. This Catacomb gravestone is not colored hence the legibility of its symbols, letters, and *guide lines* depends on light and cast shadows. The self-evident point in these and *other* inscriptions is that the sign writer wrote letter strokes and stem ends *above, below,* and *across* head and base lines,

27

which strokes he then chiselled, thus contradicting those who tell us that chisel-scratched guide lines 'defined the tops and bottoms of letter strokes and these defined ends eventually evolved into serifs.'

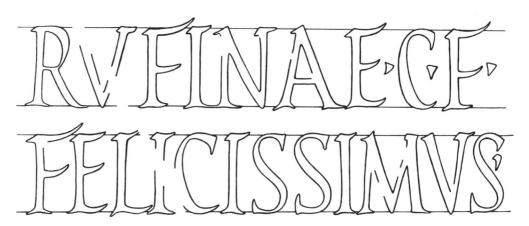

Fig. 31. *First century inscription with chisel-scratched head and base lines (1/3 size). Vatican Lapidary Galleries.*

Fig. 32. *An early Christian epitaph from the Catacomb of Pretestatus with chisel-scratched lines.*

7

What is not explained

Despite the weight of opinion behind the "chisel" theory there are many things it does not and cannot explain. Let us examine ancient letters themselves, letters made during one of the significant calligraphic epochs after the invention of the serif—Roman Imperial letters—to see if there are any historical arguments against the "chisel" attribution.

1. Some Trajan letters have a very short serif or none on one side of a stem or arm, for example, letters A, C, E, F, G, L, M, R, S, T, and X.

Fig. 33. Letter parts that could be serifed.

29

Figure 33 shows Trajan letters with arrows indicating letter parts that could support serifs. Figure 34 shows these same letters with these serifs added. It is clear that if the "chisel" origin were true these letter

ACEFG
LMRTS

Fig. 34. Trajan letters with added serifs.

•

parts, since they are stem and arm endings and therefore requiring "stops," should have "chisel" serifs at these indicated locations.

•

2. Some stems are blunted where they join strokes or curves, notably A, G, M, V, and N (Fig. 35).

The outer junctures of obliques, stems and curves not only are serif-less but do not terminate in square or angled ends. According to the "chisel-origin" way of thinking these terminals should have serifs; instead they are blunted and rounded shapes, almost directly opposed both to normal serif construction and to the angled and squared end which, in the prevailing opinion of authors, the 'chisel when cutting letters prefers.'

30

Fig. 35. Rounded, outer junctures in Trajan letters.

•

3. If the chisel made a "stop" mark at the end of stems this mark

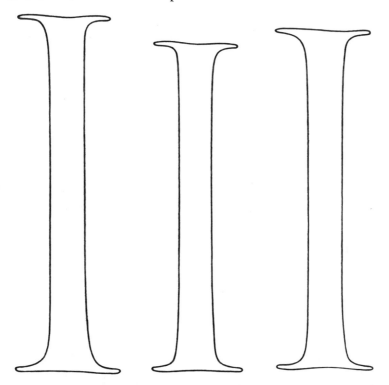

Fig. 36. Trajan I's with ox-bow curves at stem ends (3/4).

31

would be straight across the stem end. But this is not true. The fact is the outer edge of head- and foot-serifs is quite often an ox-bow curve.

•

4. The "chisel" theory offers no explanation for the dent between left and right head- and foot- serifs; between head-serifs and lobe curves in B, D, P, and R, and between serifs and arms in E, F, and L.

Fig. 37. Dents in Trajan letters.

Fig. 38. Dents in letters taken from an inscription cut during Emperor Vespasian's reign, now in the Vatican Lapidary Galleries (1/2).

32

5. Some authors tell us that serifs were balanced on either side of basic strokes. But no explanation accounts for the inequality of serif widths in letters V and X.

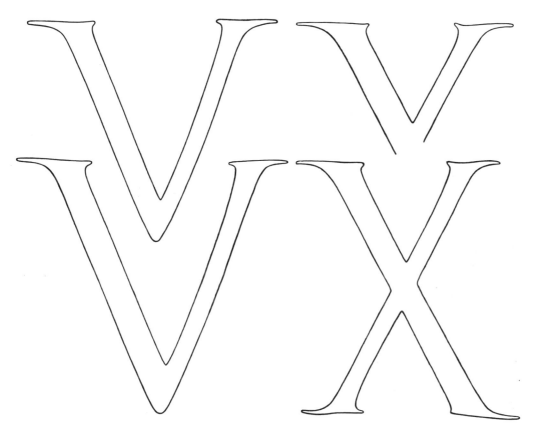

Fig. 39. Unequal left and right head-serifs in Trajan letters V and X.

•

6. Moreover, some Trajan and other Imperial foot-serifs are not perpendicular to the stem nor do they parallel the horizontal writing line, rather they point down and to the right. It would seem that if stem "stops" had been made these would have been perpendicular to the stems and parallel to the bottom writing line.

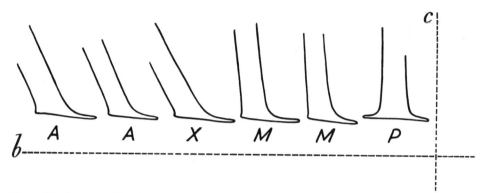

Fig. 40. Some Trajan foot-serifs in their normal vertical-horizontal (lines a, c) positions.

•

7. The lobe curves of B, D, P, and R do not begin as a straight line from the head- and foot-serif of stems. Instead they rise above and fall below the stem and its serif, indicating that neither guide lines nor "stops" had active parts in shaping these curves.

BDPR

Fig. 41. Curves of B, D, P, and R, rising above and ending below stems.

•

8. Internal junctures of stems, arms, obliques, and curves are angular in A, F, G, M, N, P, Q, R, S, T, V, and X. However, there are four letters, B, D, E, and L, which have large, rounded junctures of stem and bottom arm. Since there is but one juncture (rounded) in L, this could

34

be dismissed as a stylistic mannerism or a carry-over of a traditional usage from earlier ages. But turning to the other letters, B, D, and E, we note that each has several arms juncturing with the stem and that

Fig. 42. Angular upper junctures in B, D, and E, and rounded bottom junctures in B, D, E, and L.

all upper junctures with the stem are angular whereas the bottom is rounded. What is the reason for three angular, upper junctures and one rounded, bottom juncture in letters B, and E, and why is it that only the bottom juncture of B, D, E, and L is rounded?

•

9. The internal curves of round letters C, D, G, Q, etc., are rounded. How explain the internal rounded angle of lobe and mid-arm in

Fig. 43. The internal angles of B and R.

35

letters B, and R? Figure 44 shows smooth (letter O) and angular (B and R) inner curves of three letters taken from a first century Vatican inscription.

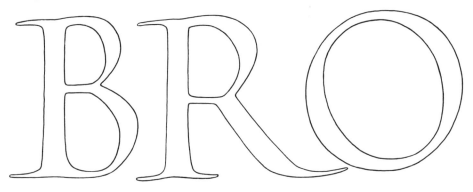

Fig. 44. Three letters from a first century inscription now in the Vatican Lapidary Galleries (1/2).

•

10. And why did the Trajan cutter waste time adding fillets? Letters lacking fillets are not ugly, nor necessarily tasteless. Without doubt

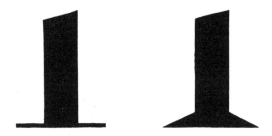

Fig. 45. Fillet-less serifs.

any of the fine Imperial lettering masters, confronted with the problem, could have designed acceptable capitals without fillets.

•

11. Moreover if the "stop" and "scratched line" theories were true they still would not explain the curved fillet. It would seem that

36

since both of these theories rely on straight cuts across stem ends, then any enlargement of serif into stem would itself be straight—as in figure 45.

•

12. Why was the serif not adopted by the Greek inscription makers who were cutting beautiful letters some centuries before the Romans—and who, like the Romans, did most of their letter cutting in marble? One could further ask why earlier cultures, Chinese, Egyptian, Indian, Sumerian, Assyrian, and others did not produce such a distinctive item as the serif in their stone-cut characters? After all, these cultures had craftsmen no less skilled than the Roman stone cutters and, like the Romans, were faced with similar stone-cutting problems. The

Fig. 46. Greek inscription (447-446 B.C.) now in the National Epigraphic Museum at Athens. Inv. No. 6769, I.G., I², 354. Actual size.

37

illustration in figure 46 is of an inscription now in the National Museum of Athens, cut in the year 447 or 446 B.C. at the very height of classic Greek art during the age of Pericles. This is not a beginner's amateurish attempt at letter making. It is in the rigid, main stem of a fixed tradition of fine Greek letter-cutting. It has no serifs.

I examined many inscriptions during research periods at the National Epigraphic Museum at Athens. What first strikes the student of Latin epigraphy, when he comes to Greek inscriptions in stone, is the general small size of the letters and the length of the inscriptions. It is not unusual to find entire inscriptions whose body text is made up of

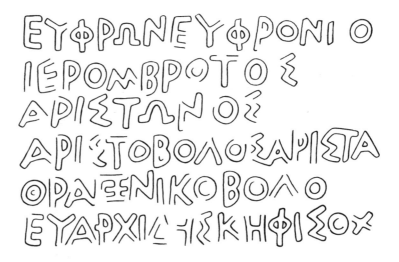

Fig. 47. Actual size of several lines from a lengthy, fourth-century (400-380 B.C. ca.) inscription now in the National Epigraphic Museum, Athens, I.G. 11², 1951.

letters one-half inch tall. In his book, *Inscriptiones Graecae* (Bonn: A. Marcus & E. Weber, 1913), Otto Kern shows several of these lengthy inscriptions from the National Museum. For example, his plate 19 illustrates an inscription cut in 405-402 B.C., having 76 lines, each line containing approximately 60 letters ¼″ tall, and plate 25 shows an inscription fragment cut about 345 B.C. of at least three columns, with each column made up of about 60 lines and each line averaging 40 letters 1/5" in height. In the epigraphic collection at Athens, Greek letters taller than two inches are scarce, and letters four or more inches tall extremely rare, whereas such letter heights were quite common in Roman inscriptions; for example, the letters in the Trajan Inscription are 3.6" to 5.2" tall.

Examination of chisel strokes in classic Greek inscriptions convinces me that the Greek calligrapher was very fast in cutting letters. This is explained partly by the vast number of letters that were being cut, which called for speed, by the method of cutting, and by the fact that the letter cutter most often did not bother to tidy up chisel cuts, especially at stem endings.

Serifs as an adjunct to large letters are not misplaced. But serifs added to small stone-cut letters, say, letters less than an inch tall, would definitely be an impediment to legibility for, even though carefully made, such serifs could easily be misread as parts of letters. Moreover the time needed to add serifs to small letters would be proportionally greater than the time required making serifs for larger letters and, considering the length of many Greek inscriptions and the vast amount of letter-cutting, would mean a proportionately greater over-all time expended. Hence the preference (until better reasons are assigned) in the classic Greek age for serif-less letters.

Besides, there are other, more remote reasons for the absence of serifs in classic letters. I have not made an exhaustive inquiry into the Greek manner of writing classic inscriptions but I am convinced that the Greek calligrapher, unlike the Roman, did not commonly use a brush or square-edged reed in writing his inscriptions. Instead I suspect that Greek calligraphers used a frayed, blunted reed, in much the same manner as that with which he wrote monolined letters on papyrus. With almost the same stroke thickness throughout the letter, no serif was needed. Had the Greek calligrapher attempted a serif with his blunt, 'stilographic' tool the result would have been, not the termination we

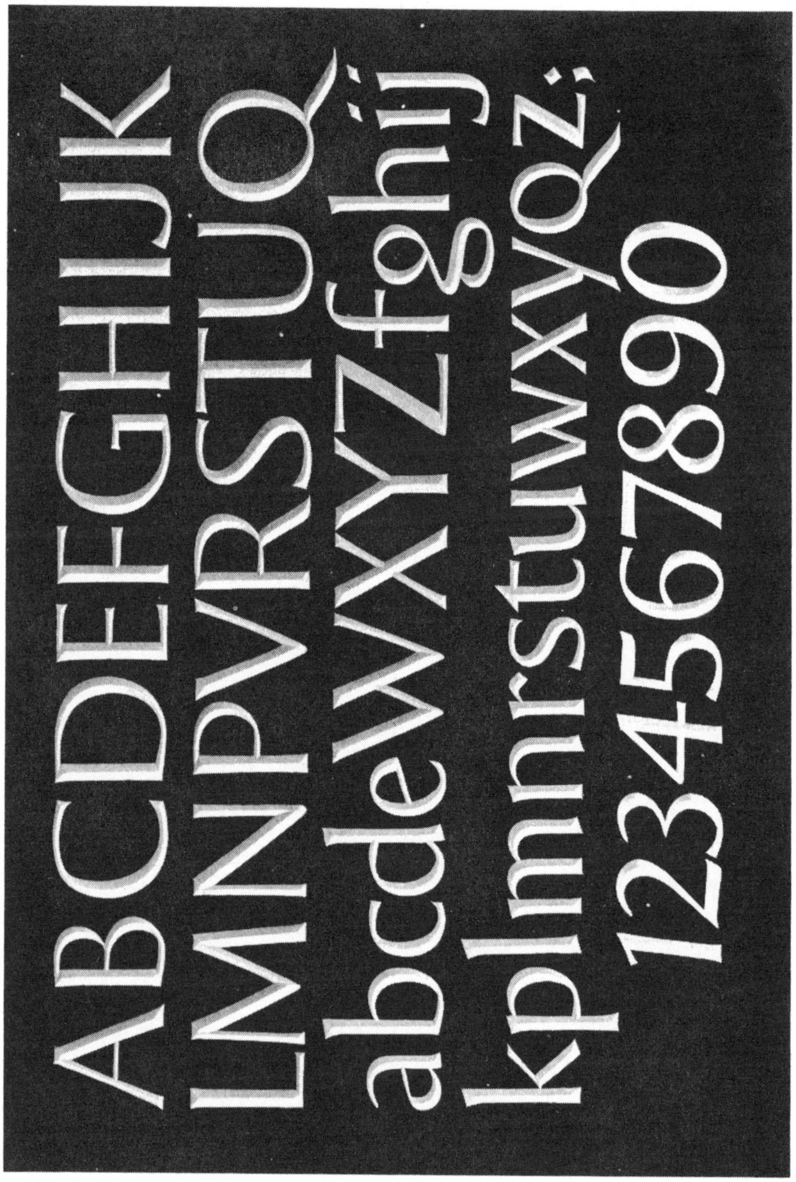

Fig. 48. A serif-less alphabet cut in stone.

40

generally associate with the serif, but a 'letter part' added to the end of a stroke.

Furthermore, from squeezes of classic Greek inscriptions which I have made, the evidence is firm that even in cutting small letters the Greek cutter employed a method that differed radically from the Roman one and this method definitely militated against serif production. Later, in the Hellenistic Age, however, long and bracketed serifs do materialize in large Greek letters. These serifs are adventitious, however. They do not appear to be dynamically determined by an inner necessity of letter making as is the case with the Roman letter and its serif.

Moreover, a glance at figures 46 and 47 seems to disprove the statements of authors who tell us that 'coming into the end of stems with the chisel tends to widen the stem-end into a serif.'

•

13. The inter-point (word separator or punctuation mark) is the least of the characters in the Trajan Inscription yet it, too, offers decisive evidence against the "chisel" theory.

MPVIXPPVFILDIV AVGGERMDACIE

Fig. 49. No spacing between Latin words.

•

In the Trajan Inscription there are 28 of these word-separating marks, which look superficially like triangles. In classical writing and lettering, words were run together with no space between words. The inter-point, slightly above center usually, and sometimes within letters, separated words and abbreviations from each other.

Any simple shape—dot, diamond, round, or square—could have

been used. The *easiest* and quickest shape to chisel in stone is a triangle. And in fact this was the approach essayed by a first century letter-cutter

Fig. 50. *Inter-points as word separators.*

•

from Puteoli who made two chisel cuts from each corner of a triangle and did not bother to line up the three sides of the triangle. His finished inter-points look like three-rayed stars.

Fig. 51. *'Triangular' inter-points from a Puteoli inscription now in the National Museum of Naples. First century. Full size.*

•

Two orientations for a triangle suggest themselves—with the point up or down, and with base parallel to the writing line.

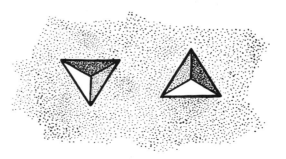

Fig. 52. *Triangles cut in stone.*

42

But in the Trajan Inscription these inter-points have their *bases up* only and *inclined* consistently to the *left* at about twenty-five degrees from the horizontal. The inclined base is straight, but oddly, the other two sides are curved and both point to the left.

Fig. 53. Six inter-points from various lines
in the Trajan Inscription. Full size.

•

If the "chisel" interpretation were true the base (either up or down) of the inter-point would parallel the writing lines, all three sides would incline neither to left nor right, and all three angles would generally be equal. Clearly the "chisel" theory for the origin of the serif cannot stand up.

43

8

Reed-pen, 2-pencil theories

et us examine the suggestions that the reed-pen and the two joined pencils account for letter formation in the inscription alphabet. Some writers suggest that the preliminary layout for Roman inscription letters was made with a large reed or by a marking device such as two pencils tied together and held at a constant cant thus producing the character-

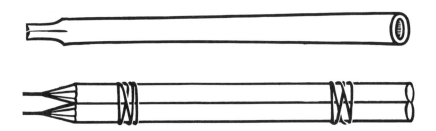

Fig. 54. Reed and two joined pencils.

•

istic thicks, thins, and swells, as well as serifs, of the Roman alphabet. I quote from some of these theorists:

•

The pen, probably more than any other tool, has had the strongest influence upon lettering in respect of serif design, owing to the inflexible nature of its manipulation, and the constantly held oblique angle at which it is usually held.

L. C. Evetts, A.R.C.A., *Roman Lettering* (New York: Pitman, 1938), p. 3.

•

. . . other vestiges of the pen are the upper serifs of T both pointing to the left . . .

•

He made his (Trajan) N's with three thick strokes, and this again suggests pen construction.

Ibid., p. 3.

•

The double lines so produced (by the 2-pencil marker) form the outside bounds of the letters which are completed by filling-in with a pen or brush.

Oscar Ogg, *An Alphabet Source Book,* p. 39.

•

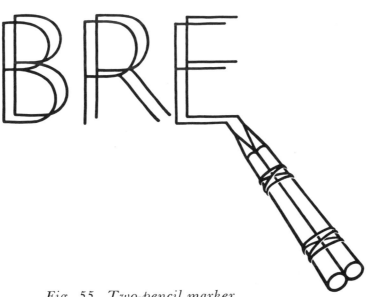

Fig. 55. Two-pencil marker.

•

. . . it is generally agreed . . . the letters were not incised direct, but were . . . first planned by a hand using a broad, or manuscript pen.

Russell Laker, *The Anatomy of Lettering, p. 8.*

•

The shapes they take in general and their proportions are, therefore, those of pen-drawn letters . . .

Frederic W. Goudy, *The Alphabet and Elements of Lettering* (Berkeley: University of California Press, 1942), p. 42.

•

An interesting development in the letter-forms of Roman capitals took place about 154 B.C. This was the introduction of serifs— probably due to the influence of writing with broad-pointed reed or quill pen and ink on papyrus.

Harold Deighton, *The Art of Lettering* (London: B. T. Batsford, 1947), p. 10.

•

From the shapes of letters (Trajan), it is obvious that they were written on the slab itself with a broad reed pen, and then cut in with the chisel.

Allen W. Seaby, *The Roman Alphabet and its Derivations* (London: B. T. Batsford, Ltd., 1925), p. 6.

•

. . . the inscription (Trajan) gives clear evidence of an early use of the broad pen . . .

•

46

But the following objections to the reed pen and 2-pencil theories immediately arise:

1. Parts of Roman letters are thinner or thicker than a reed or 2-pencil marking device would normally make. For example, there is a slight swelling where stems merge into fillets and serifs. There is a thickening at the bottom of the tail in letter R and the oblique of letter S.

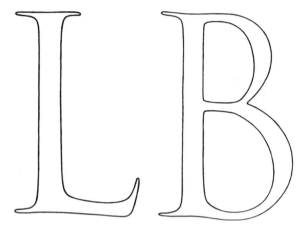

Fig. 56. Variations in stem and lobe thickness.

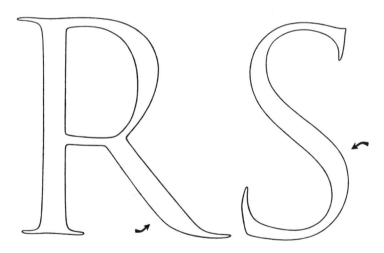

Fig. 57. Swells in R and S.

47

2. The lobes of inscription B, D, P, and R are quite difficult to make with the reed. The radical changes of cant within these lobes is not typical of a reed or 2-pencil marking tool. In figure 58 cross lines show changes in cant that would be necessary to produce the strokes of the Imperial inscription R and P.

Fig. 58. Changes of cant in letter R.

•

3. The top lobe of B, and sometimes P, and R, is thinner in its greatest width than the normal mark made by the reed or 2-pencil designing tool. (cf. figs. 107, 111, 116, 121, 209).

Fig. 59. Lobes in B, P, and R.

48

4. The reed-pen serif-theory disagrees with the serifs in the Trajan Inscription. The top three letters in figure 60 show normal reed serifs while below them are the corresponding Trajan letters.

MTN

MTN

Fig. 60. Reed and Trajan serifs.

Figure 61 shows some arm serifs that can be made for reed-written letters F and S. These arm serifs would apply as well to C, G, E, and T But none of these resemble the inscription serif.

F≡ S≋

Fig. 61. Reed-written arm serifs for letters F, S, C, E, G, and T

49

•

5. Finally, besides serifs, many parts of inscription letters do not echo similar shapes made by the reed, for example, the arms of C, D, S, the oblique junctures of A, M, N, V, the arms of E, F, L, T, etc.

TGNVES
TGNVES

Fig. 62. A comparison of reed-written and inscription letters.

•

6. There is another explanation for serifs by those who say that stem ends in Roman stonecut letters should be heavier for esthetic reasons and that serifs provide this esthetic effect. The proposal that stem

Fig. 63. Thickened stem ends.

50

ends be emphasized in some manner over stem shafts is valid. But is it necessary that broad serifs with fillets be introduced for this esthetic effect? Surely a simple, easily made widening of the stem end would be sufficient. And indeed this may well have been in the mind of the Greek

Fig. 64. The 41st Oration of Demosthenes cut by Praxiteles, fourth century B.C., now in the restored Stoa of the American School for Classical Studies at Athens. Full size.

51

sculptor Praxiteles (whose productive life ranged from 375 to about 330 B.C.), when he cut such an inscription (Fig. 64). And this solution would not have been beyond the calligraphic inventiveness of the Imperial Roman writing and lettering masters three, four and five centuries later and who, moreover, undoubtedly were familiar with the solution produced by Praxiteles and other Greek letterers.

•

7. There is at least one author who asserts that the serif is not Roman but Greek in origin. Up to a certain point this is true, that is, if we choose to see no difference between Greek and Roman serifs, or if we ignore the serif's inner causality. Actually if one is guided by appearances one could go beyond the Greeks and suggest Babylonian Cuneiform as having harbored the germ of a serif. In figure 65 the two letters on the left, taken from the 41st Oration of Demosthenes and cut in mar-

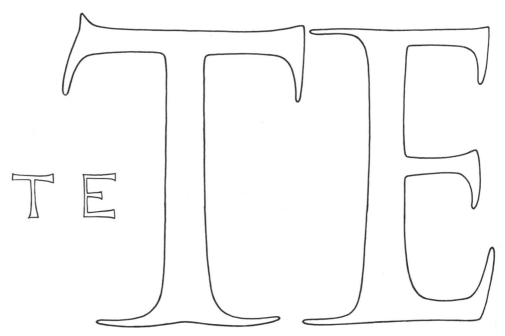

Fig. 65. Fourth century B.C. Greek letters and first century Roman letters. Full size.

52

ble by Praxiteles, were made up of strokes of equal width. He widened these strokes slightly at their ends for esthetic reasons and thus produced a kind of serif.

In the third century the influence of Greek ideas on Roman minds was so strong, as expressed in the tag "Greece conquered led Rome captive," that these Greek stem endings have been taken to be the origin of the Roman serif. The appearance of a Greek type of serif in Latin letters in the third century B.C.[1], would at first sight seem to support this opinion. I am convinced, however, that such an attribution is quite mistaken. The Greek serif was extraneous. It was not an integral part of the Greek letter as is the Roman serif. Moreover Rome's singular invention of shaded writing, Roman writing tools, cutting methods, and the use of much taller letters of dissimilar character resulted in a Roman serif quite different from the Greek one. The broad, treacly, bracketed, ox-bow-shaped, Imperial Roman serif is *unique*. It had no antecedent.

•

8. Finally there is a class of authors who suggest that Imperial letterers made use of double line layout, building-up, filling-in, stencils or pattern letters before chiselling the inscriptional letters. I list some of them and their assertions:

•

Quite distinct, however, from the abruptness of pen-made curves, the change from thick to thin portions in all the round letters is exceedingly subtle, and peculiar in design to tools which produce letters of built-up character.

The chief difference between inscriptional characters and MS. letters lies in the fact that stone-cut forms are . . . built up, part at a time, and not made by single sweeping strokes of a pen or brush.

L. C. Evetts, A.R.C.A., *Roman Lettering*, p. 13.

•

53

. . . show indications that the letters were carefully outlined or painted in before cutting . . .

Frederic W. Goudy, *The Alphabet and Elements of Lettering,* p. 42.

●

This standard *scriptura monumentalis* was mainly the work of the professional stone-cutter, who made the letters with exactness after a pattern previously outlined in color or crayon.

James C. Egbert, *Introduction to the Study of Latin Inscriptions* (New York American Book Co., 1896), p. 37.

●

There is no indication of free 'hand and eye' planning in the 'lay-out' as a whole, 'elasticity,' in the treatment of the (Trajan) letters, being entirely absent.

Harold Deighton, *The Art of Lettering,* p. 39.

●

Thus [Trajan] letters of the same size are so stereotyped and alike in effect that this could only be obtained by drawing-like copying.

Walter Kaech, *Rhythm and Proportion in Lettering* (Olten, Switzerland: Verlag Otto Walter, 1956), p. 37.

●

We need not devote much time to refuting double-line layout, building-up, outlining, the use of stencils or pattern letters, etc. The nature of fine Imperial letters simply excluded such methods. For example, in each of the six lines of the Trajan Inscription some letters as A, D, E, I, M, N, O, P, R, S, T, V, and X are repeated. The better Imperial letters maintain their height-to-width relationships and were not purposely extended or condensed to fit the line. Accordingly, if pat-

terns had been used one should expect to find like letters from the same
line in the Trajan Inscription (since they are of the same height) to
match over each other. Figures 66 and 67 shows some of these superimposed, paired letters from the same line in the Inscription. These outline letters, reduced one-third, are taken from the portfolio, *Letters
Redrawn from the Trajan Inscription in Rome,* mentioned earlier.
Breaks in letter outline indicate damage to the original letter in Rome.
The list below shows to which line paired letters belong, Numbers under BLACK and GRAY indicate which letters of the same line are used,
e.g., the 1st and 2nd R of the second line, the 2nd and 4th D of the fifth
line, etc.

LETTER	LINE	BLACK	GRAY
R	2	1	2
T	3	2	1
D	5	2	4
S	1	1	4
T	6	4	1
O	3	1	2
S	6	1	5
A	5	1	2
E	6	3	1

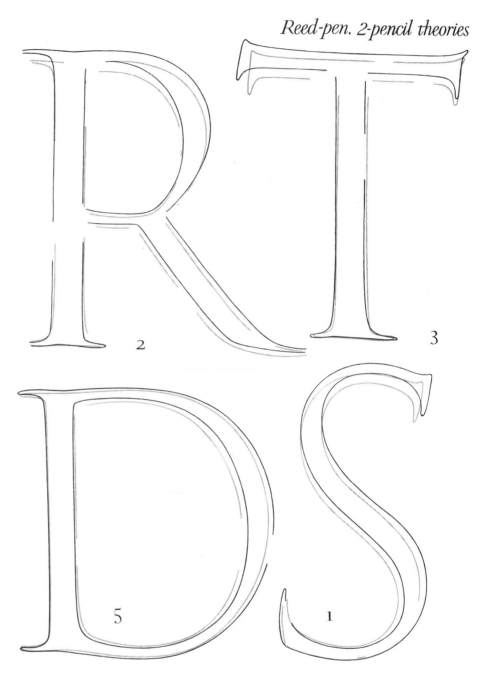

Fig. 66. *Superimposed letters, 2/3 of original size, from the 1st, 2nd, 3rd, and 5th lines of the Trajan Inscription, disproving the use of stencils or patterns.*

56

Fig. 67. Superimposed letters from the 3rd, 5th and 6th lines of the Trajan Inscription, 2/3 of original size.

57

Figure 68 shows inter-points from five of the six lines in the Trajan Inscription. The number under each point indicates the line to which it belongs. The vertical-horizontal alignment of these points in figure 68 is identical with the alignment each point has in the Inscription. Eight of these points are taken from the fourth line. It is apparent that no two of these are geometrically alike and the difference should disprove decisively the use of outline-patterning, or stencil methods.

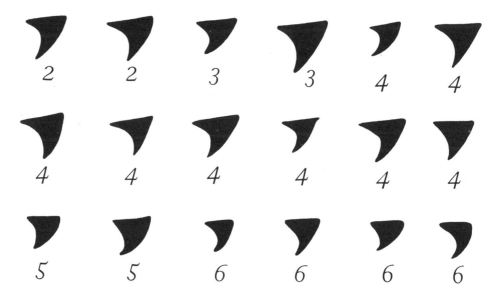

Fig. 68. Trajan inter-points from five of the six lines in the Inscription.

In addition ancient calligraphic skill and speed indirectly argue against the use of patterns, outlining, etc. In the late Republic and early Empire, book publishing was a large industry. Books were plentiful and public libraries date from the first century B.C. Libraries for Greek and Latin works were founded by Augustus and later by Vespasian. In the post-Augustan age, Rome had 28 public libraries, the most magnificent being Trajan's *Bibliotheca Ulpia,* with large Greek and Latin branches. Of course there were many private libraries and book collections. We know that entire libraries were among the war spoils which Sulla (138-78 B.C.), Lucullus, and others, gathered in the East and in Greece and brought to Rome.

In Rome there were no printed books, typewriters, tape recorders, or standardized shorthand systems. But there was a vast amount of writing, for whatever was published and read was hand written. The writing speed of the educated Roman may surprise us. Cicero tells of Roman senators able to take dictated evidence verbatim. Martial indicates that his second book of Epigrams, containing 540 verses, could be copied by a scribe[2] in an hour (". . . quod haec una peragit librarius hora, . .") that is, nine verses or about 200 letters per minute. If Martial's expert copyist had such speed, it hardly seems believable that trained *librarii*, turned inscription makers (sign writers), would dawdle over an inscription layout by filling-in, outlining, or using similar slow lettering techniques.

It would appear, then, that neither the chisel, scratched guide lines, reed, 2-pencil, patterns, ornamental, esthetic reason nor outlining methods explain the origin of the serif and the shapes of Roman letters. In all these proposals the weakness is that they are not supported by evidence. An acceptable theory should:

1. embrace *all* known Imperial letter parts and serifs;

2. be readily demonstrable in ordinary practice;

3. apply equally well to all classes and kinds of Imperial inscriptions, *scriptura actuaria* as well as *scriptura monumentalis*.

9

Chiselled V-cuts

We now leave our discussion on the serif for 67 pages, in what may appear to be a set of unrelated digressions, in order to take up inscription making in stone. This 'digression' material is pertinent, and very important, as will be seen when later we return to our central theme. We will here discuss the chiselled V-cut, what purpose it serves, the painting of V-cuts, shadows in stone-cut letters, lettering methods in stone, the antecedence of reed over chisel, reed writing, the primacy of writing over lettering, and other related matters.

Since the chiseled V-cut underlies much that we are discussing, we must study some of its history, nature, and place in the inscription craft, in order to understand how, in recent times, false notions about V-cuts began.

Art students, tourists, and amateur archeologists, long accustomed to seeing the Parthenon, Erechtheum and classic Greek sculpture in their clean, white marble, forget, or overlook, the fact that originally these were painted over in color. As an example, Praxiteles used the encaustic method to tint the flesh and color the hair, eyes and drapery of his statue "Aphrodite of Cnidus" now in the Vatican Sculpture Gallery. In fact all Greek sculpture whether terra-cotta, limestone, wood, or marble, was painted. The Greeks derived this technique from the Egyptians and passed it on to the Romans and, eventually, to medieval craftsmen.

The rediscovery of weathered, often broken, classical Greek works of art in the Renaissance fixed in cultivated minds from that time onwards, the idea that marble statuary should be left in its natural color with neither polychrome nor gilding.

60

Renaissance sculptors, bemused by the "Cult-of-the-Antique" and lacking the archeological knowledge of ancient practices that we possess today, apparently believed that the Greek sculptor intended an unadorned statue. The anti-Gothic reaction against painted and gilded wood and stone sculpture still further strengthened the Renaissance sculptor's and art collector's 'clean marble' attitude.

Much rediscovered Greek statuary was excavated, hence it was caked with soil and crusts. The mild acid used to clean it removed the dirt and chemical leachings, and, unfortunately, also any trace of paint. Without doubt, this further confirmed the view favoring unpainted sculpture[3] and, since inscriptions were mostly cut in marble, they too were affected.

This 'clean marble' concept has come down to us unchanged but not unchallenged. As it applies to inscriptions it is the first obstacle to a correct understanding of chiselled work, for it led to excessively deep V-cuts for the sake of shadows, and thus to the false 3-dimensional concept of stone-cut letters.[4]

A second obstacle is the exaggeration of the importance of tools and materials in our times. One of the major advances of art expression in the past half century has been a great increase of respect for tools, materials, and their working. No one denies that this change has enriched all the arts and crafts. However, it is not so important as to eclipse all other considerations. Like any other part of an artistic unity tools and materials must contribute their special unique good to the whole but in the right amount, time and place.

Much has been said about "not removing tool marks." Undeniably this has had a telling effect on letterers, wood carvers and sculptors. Every workman values his contribution to the composite product. This may explain why today stone letters so often are left in their original V-cutting with no adornment of color or gilding over chisel cuts.

There is still another obstacle to a realistic appreciation of stone-cut inscriptions. Cutting letters by hand on stone with mallet and chisel has virtually disappeared in our country. It has been supplanted to a great extent by sandblasting techniques, power tools, and template routers. One consequence has been to elevate practitioners of the dying craft of stone-cut lettering out of the ordinary level of craft skill to the rarefied pinnacle of "folk survival" art. This has led stone cutters to think themselves a breed apart and to evaluate their stone cutting and letter-making work as somewhat more important than it actually is.

One can readily see how it is possible to justify the raw chisel cut and to leave it as an honest, unchanged, tool-quality mark, self-sufficient in its own independent existence. Accordingly these three attitudes 1) historical, 2) technical-esthetic, and 3) "arts and crafts," combine to explain our present conviction in favor of the "clean V-cut."

The unadorned chisel mark may seem to be a minor issue. Actually it is important. One would not be far wrong to say that it has debased the whole contemporary concept of inscription making. It has given the stone letter-cutting craftsman exaggerated notions of his own importance, has given us false ideas of Imperial writing and lettering, and has altered our standards of how letters should look. As we shall see, this neo-primitivism has far-reaching consequences for our central inquiry into serifs and the nature of Roman letters.

10

Painting V-cuts

ow the significant, external mark that sets off the craft of the inscription cutter is the chiselled V-cut. The cutter can hardly be blamed if he allows his V-cut to stand alone, unadorned. Cut letters, if gilded or painted, tend to fall from their unique position as part of an ancient, all-but-forgotten craft, and become part of the common sign painter's domain, there to serve along with neon, plastic, sheet metal, and gold leaf signs—merely as one among many.

It may shock stone letterers to be told that, historically considered, the V-cutting of letters is merely one of several steps to the completion of the inscription sequence; that the V-cut is a means and not an end; that the V-cut is but the basis for painting or gilding. To prove the point let us look for a moment at the Trajan Inscription and Column in Rome.

Many, even some art historians and teachers, are not aware that originally the entire Trajan Column from top to bottom (including the near-800-foot long spiral bas-relief scroll that makes 23 turns from base to Column top) was polychromed. On the underside of the abacus one can see traces of green, blue, red, and gilt. The Column was surmounted by a *gilded* bronze statue of the Emperor Trajan. Traces of various colors can be seen in the long scroll and particles of red-orange coloring are still visible in the letters of the Inscription at the Column's base.

As a rule Roman inscriptions, even the ancient ones, after being cut were painted with red-orange pigment, usually *minium* (red oxide of lead, that is, Pb_3O_4) or red mercuric sulphide, (vermilion, that is, HgS). Pliny mentions this (H. N. xxxiii, 122; "... minium in voluminum quoque scriptura usurpatur clarioresque litteras vel in aere (Mommsen in muro) vel in marmore etiam in sepulcris facit.'') That is, 'vermilion is used for bookhand script; moreover it makes clearly legible letters on walls (bronze) and marble, even tombs.'

11

Purpose V-cut serves

ventually the question will suggest itself; if it is true that V-cuts were promptly painted over as soon as they were chiselled, what purpose, then, did the chiselled V-cut serve?

The answer is that the V-cut helped to preserve the original writing of the inscription. Chiselling is the shield protecting the fragile writing from its natural enemies, abrasion and erasure by windblown sand, by sun and rain. The ancients knew that surface writing on stone was easily and quickly effaced.

In proof, we look again at the Trajan Inscription, written, chiselled, and painted eighteen and a half centuries ago. One-half of the projecting cornice which protected the Inscription has been broken away. The extreme left third and right sixth of this protective cornice is still intact. The letters underneath the broken-out portion of the cornice are most eroded and damaged. Those areas on the left and right ends of the Inscription, through the centuries protected by the cornice, give us letters today that are sharper, better preserved and more informative. Without doubt, then, the function of the overhanging cornice is to *preserve the letters* from damage and effacement.

Now cutting the inscription letters into the stone puts them beyond those weathering agencies of rain, hail, wind, and sun, ever working to erase them. This practice was not peculiar to the Romans. It was commonly used by the earlier Sumerians, Assyrians, and Egyptians. In effect, then, *chiselling* is insurance, a *protective cornice* for the survival of inscriptions.

Chiselling therefore is wholly ancillary to writing and lettering. It is the supporting buttress to the written inscription which is the all-important element. But the 'cornice' is meaningless if what it protects can be seen only with difficulty — hence the need for painting the 'cornice.'

The whole inscription-making process evolved easily, naturally and simply. First came the writing on the stone, next the V-cut, chiselling away the writing and thus 'cornicing' it into the stone, and finally the repainting of the V-cut to restore the original writing — that is, 1) writing; 2) chiselling; 3) painting.

Making a comparison with the craft of enameling one can say that the chiselled V-cut stands in the same relationship to the inscription it carries that the cloison (cell partition) has to the colored enamel it

Fig. 69. The Trajan Inscription in Rome showing the cornice (and its broken out section) that originally protected the chiselled letters.

66

holds. Deprive this cell of its coloring enamel and serious damage is done to the design. Take away the re-painting from chiselled letters and a like damage results. Unpainted, chisel-cut letters are as unnatural as cloisons without enamel.

Fig. 70. A photograph taken in 1897 before the Trajan Inscription was scrubbed with acid to remove the weather staining, moss, and soil crusts caused by the broken-out section of the projecting cornice. The acid cleansing was done in the interest of the tourist trade.

67

Fig. 71. The Trajan Inscription as it appears today.

68

12

Strength generally triumphs not only in the arena of action but in the region of ideas. That is, in any union or confront- ation, it is usually the stronger that prevails. The traits of the dominant tend to overshadow those of the sub-domi- nant. In the realm of ideas the more readily understood characteristics of either of two related ideas tend to color both. Suggest one and you call the other to mind with the result that the attributes and prerogatives of both are apt to be inter-mixed.

It is difficult to disassociate stone-cut lettering from sculpture. Both crafts work on stone, using much the same techniques with common tools and methods — mallets and chisels, forgings and sharpenings. The usual notion is that there is an inseparable bond between the two, and that what is true of one is true of the other. The union of crafts is further strengthened by the knowledge that the most widely publicized stone-letterer of our century, Eric Gill, was a fine stone sculptor.

Stone-lettering, today, is an arcane craft (even to most calligraphers whose business is making letters) whereas the craft of sculpture is widely and easily understood. But stone sculpture, above all, is 3-dimensional and this characteristic tends to attribute to incised letters a like quality. This transference of traits, without doubt, has had a disruptive influ- ence both without and within the craft of stone-cut lettering.

One consequence, plainly evident in our time, is that too much value is assigned to the chiselled V-cut so that the 3-dimensional V-cut becomes an end in itself. To be sure the V-cut is necessary, but only as a means. A craftsman making only the V-cut may be likened to the sign painter who, having made the outlines of letters, looks at them, sees that they are visually weak, and proceeds to fatten the outlines to bring

69

the letter out — instead of filling-in the outlines so that the *whole letter* will bear the burden of legibility.

Stone-cut lettering, having unwittingly assumed sculpture's 3-dimensional character, gravitates towards the third dimension of light and shade. Shadows become important and hence it is natural to emphasize them. But, unfortunately, when chisel cutting is made an end, stone letterers tend to see their stone-cut letters as solid, 3-dimensional quantities having lights and shadows. The demand then is for deeper V-cuts in order to bring out heavier shadows. This attitude has not been helped by those calligraphic theorists who write lettering books. Witness the following quotations:

●

. . . the shadow cast by the upper portions of the swells would add to the apparent weight of the curves . . .

Frederic W. Goudy, *The Capitals from the Trajan Inscription in Rome,* p. 9.

●

. . . the hair-line of the bowl at top is lighter in D as the cutter feared the greater length of line would gather too much shadow . . .

Ibid., p. 31.

●

To make their letter carry by shadows, the Roman stone cutters sometimes cut their outlines very wide.

Thomas Wood Stevens, *Lettering,* p. 28.

●

And because you cannot draw a V-shaped incision in stone to a square end that will define itself by its shadow, as a monumental letter must do . . .

Ibid., p. 27.

70

. . . this letter [Trajan] was cut with V section in marble and placed in a situation where strong sunlight would produce high lights and strong shadows . . .

John R. Biggs, *The Craft of Lettering* (London: Blandford Press, 1961), p. 6.

•

It is true that V-cut letters, lacking the definition of paint, are contrasted in their parts by the lights and shadows of the V-cuts. In that case since the shadow bears the responsibility for the inscription's legibility it is clear why the letterer, in order to get strong shadows, must make deep V-cuts. But is this enough? No respectable sign painter would think of attaching wooden, block-letters to a sign board, leaving both board and letters in their natural, wood color, for this would put the burden of legibility entirely on the shadows cast by the block-letters. Yet much the same thing occurs when the stone cutter considers his sunken

Fig. 72. Optimum V-cut shadows.

71

letters finished (though neither painted nor gilded), and thus having the necessary contrast for quick and easy reading of the inscription.

Light conditions vary. Under some conditions it is possible to have optimum light from the correct angle giving a favorable contrast of shadow and light. But some inscriptions are so placed, even in good light, as never to get the correct light angle for viewing the shadows of their letters.

The best orientation for chiselled V-cut letters would provide a strong light from above and the side, say in the noon sun. In such a position and time the high-lighted side, opposite the shadow side, would also have a value contrast from the face of the stone which receives a slanted, and therefore less, light. Even so placed, however, early morning, late afternoon, and cloudy days will produce weak shadows detrimental to legibility. When the light source is directly in front of the inscription, both sides of the V-cut will receive equal lighting, thus reducing still further the contrast needed for legibility. Considering the variables in lighting, it would seem that too great a burden is placed on cast shadows.

Quite often the lighted side of the letter's V-cut has practically the same color and value as the face of the stone, since both receive the same amount of light. The dark or shaded side of the V-cut is then the chief means contrasting the cut letter with the remainder of the stone. Since the shaded side is but *one-half of the whole V-cut* it is apparent that letters must be fattened to achieve normal readability. This is the reason why many contemporary letterers design and cut "chubby" Roman letters in which thin parts are thicker than they need be.

•

. . . as they [Trajan letters] make their effect by light and shade, they were cut more widely than appears. All incised letters are treated thus.

Allen W. Seaby, *The Roman Alphabet and its Derivatives* (London: B. T. Batsford, Ltd., 1925), p. 4.

•

72

In stone-cut letters, on the other hand, where the shadows rather than the outlines themselves reveal the forms, different limitations govern the problem. The thin lines of a letter to be V-sunk should generally be made slightly thicker in proportion to the wide lines than is the case with pen-drawn letters . . .

Frank Chouteau Brown, *Letters & Lettering* (Boston: Bates & Guild Co., 1921), p. 10.

●

This concern for shadows reveals why cutters, here and abroad, in order to make their incised letters legible, find it necessary to cut very deep V-cuts of sixty or more degrees and to thicken normally thin letter parts.

One suspects that commercial considerations, in good measure, underlie today's sandblasted lettering technique. Sandblasting has one good point. The technique produces an uneven bottom in the channel

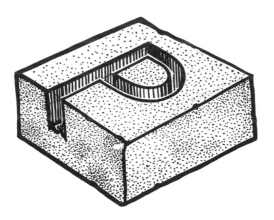

Fig. 73. Sandblasted letter.

●

blasted out. In order to conceal this unevenly blasted bottom, letters are purposely deeply bitten — so deeply that the bottom can be seen only on close inspection. The sides of the channel are perpendicular to the face of the stone and there is no V-cut to catch the light. Despite the

73

wretched quality of the stencils, the letters have the merit of greater contrast because the depth of the sandblasted cut gives a full, dark, letter shadow. But the tombstone sandblasters like the hand-letterers do not,

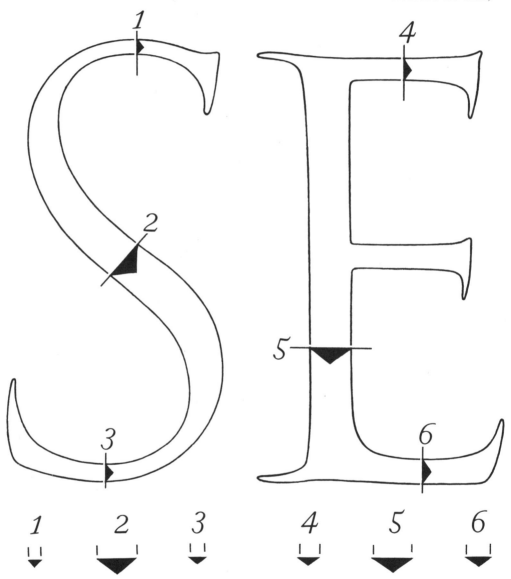

Fig. 74. The depth of V-cuts in the first two letters of the Trajan Inscription. Full size.

74

for the most part, paint or gild their cuts.

An examination of better ancient letters readily demonstrates that their makers did not depend on shadows. They designed their letters and thought of them as 2-dimensional, linear, shapes, even though *accidentally* these letters are preserved to us in 3-dimensional V-cuts. The first proof is derived from the shallowness of ancient V-cut lettering. In figure 74 are some cross sections showing depth of V-cut in the first two letters of the Trajan Inscription. The letters, and depth of V-cut, are full size.

A second proof is brought to light by the nature of the root in V-cuts of the Trajan and other Imperial letters. That is, the V-cut angle is constant so that narrow letter parts have shallow roots and wide letter parts

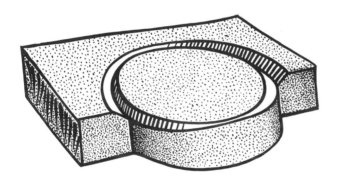

Fig. 75. The root of a Trajan letter O is a 3-dimensional space curve, not a 2-dimensional oval.

•

have deep V-cut roots. Thus the root of Trajan letter O, with its two thick and two thin curves, is a 3-dimensional space curve and not a 2-dimensional oval (Fig. 75).

The resultant shadows in Imperial letters, particularly at stroke junctures and ends, militate against "shadow" interpretation. Had Imperial cutters intended shadows to bear the burden of legibility it is inconceivable that they would have permitted the junctures and endings shown, for example, in figure 76. Indeed all upper angular joinings of

75

Fig. 76. The angular junctures of thick and thin strokes in Imperial letters having a constant V-cutting angle, and below, the shadows these letters make.

thick and thin letter parts (for example, in B, E, F, R, etc.) will be similar to the right juncture of bar and thick oblique of letter A in figure 76. The plain fact is that had the ancients really sought both shadows and a constant cutting angle they would have made deep rather than shallow V-cuts.

A much better solution, if shadows had been desired, would have been to make the roots of all V-cuts lie in the same plane below the stone's surface. Such a position would be analogous to 3-dimensional letters above the surface — in which the apex (inverted root) of all letter parts would be the same distance above the surface of the stone. In fact I am convinced that authors not familiar with stone-lettering

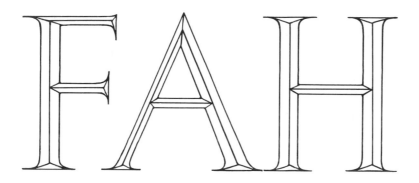

Fig. 77. 'Architectural' letters with thick and thin V-cut roots lying in the same plane.

•

think of incised letters as the reverse of raised letters in which the root of the V-cuts for thick and thin letter parts lies in a plane parallel to the surface of the stone. One need only to refer to lettering and architectural manuals showing Roman alphabets intended as models for inscriptional use on buildings. Figure 77, for example, shows letters F A H so designed.

There is no tradition or literary reference even remotely suggesting that letters were regarded as 3-dimensional.[5] Bronze letters, though solid, were meant to be read from the front like other letters. There was no reason why the scribe, traditionally thinking of and making letters as linear, 2-dimensional, graphic marks in every context, should suddenly decide, when cutting inscriptions, that his letters should then become 3-dimensional and that he therefore should be concerned about their shadows.

Deep & shallow V-cuts

I f it is true that cutting the inscription below the surface of the stone preserved the writing, should it not follow that a deep V-cut would be even better protection? The reasoning is only partly valid. As in other protective schemes, there is an area of diminishing return or needless over-protection. Thus a V-cut one inch deep is not twice as well protected as a cut one-half inch deep.

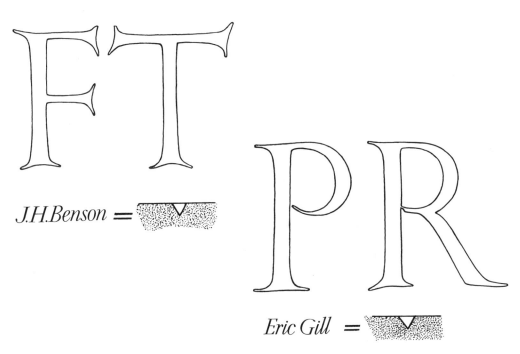

Fig. 78. Letters with their V-sections, redrawn from two alphabet stones in the Newberry Library, Chicago.

For example, the Trajan letterer had learned through long experience, or through craft tradition, how deep (Fig. 74) to make his V-cut (surprisingly shallow when compared with the V-cuts of such modern masters as Eric Gill, Will Carter, and John Benson). The fact that the Trajan Inscription is still eminently readable after eighteen and a half centuries of weathering and vandalism confirms the correctness of its shallow V-cut angle. The illustrations in figure 78 are carefully copied from rubbings and V-cut angle and depth measurements of alphabet stones cut by Eric Gill and John Benson and now in the permanent collection of the Newberry Library, Chicago.

In his tract on stone lettering Eric Gill advised a ". . . study of the best examples of Inscriptions: such as that on the Trajan Column. . ." in Appendix B to Edw. Johnston's *Writing & Lettering,* page 355. But in his own work he ignored entirely the shallow V-cutting of the Trajan Inscription. Moreover in his written instructions for stone-cut letters he said, *"For incised letters,* a "V" section of about 60° is best for regular use; deeper rather than shallower." Ibid., page 369.

Deep V-cutting has been defended in Great Britain (when I questioned the deep V-cuts) and New England on the premise that ". . . we do not have a sun as strong as that in Trajan's Rome where shallow V-cutting may have been normal." But the defense is not pertinent for it still revolves around shadows.

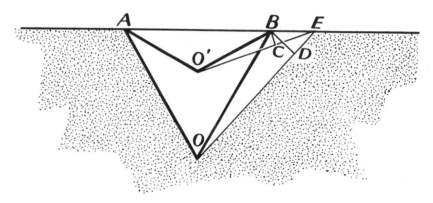

Fig. 79. A comparison of cutting mistakes in deep and shallow V-cutting.

It is easier for beginners and advanced amateurs to cut letters with deep V-cuts, but it takes more time since more stone is cut away. It is thus quicker, though more **dangerous,** to use a shallow cutting angle.

It is the edge between the V-cut and stone surface that is the cutter's goal, for this edge marks the outlines of the inscription letter. A mistake while cutting shallow V-cuts is more damaging to this letter edge than a similar mistake in deep V-cut letters. This is quite plain from the diagram in figure 79 showing shallow V-cutting (angle AO'B) and deep V-cutting (angle AOB). It is obvious that BD, the amount of error made by the chisel in deep cutting, is greater than BC, a chisel mistake in shallow cutting, yet both chisel-cutting mistakes (BC and BD) produce the same amount of surface error, BE.

It follows that it *takes more skill,* greater **control,** and sensitivity *to cut shallow V-cuts.* The skillful worker in every craft, after long experience, inevitably learns the best, surest, most efficient and *quickest* means

Fig. 80. The possibility of edge injury in deep and shallow V-cutting.

for obtaining the ends of his art, and he eliminates as well all time-wasting, unnecessary movements and methods.

Strictly speaking a shallow V-cut will stand up better against edge-injury. The steeper the angle between side and face of stone the greater

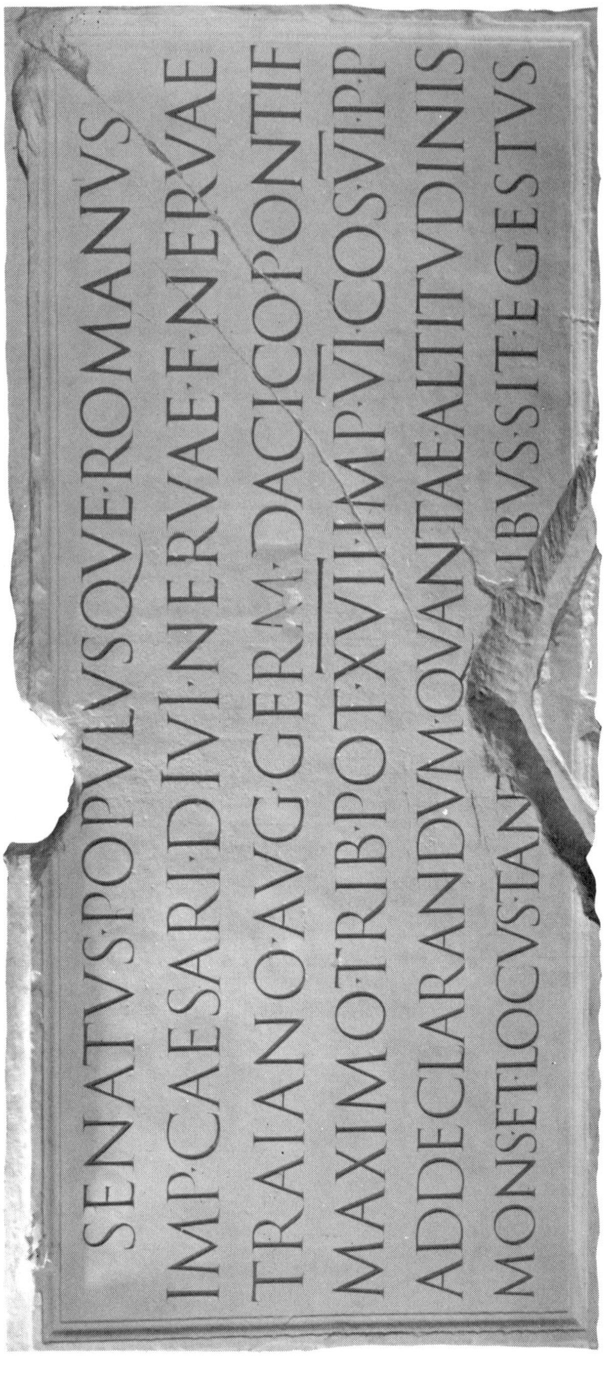

Fig. 81. The R. R. Donnelley cast of the Trajan Inscription.

the danger of chipping the edge; conversely a lesser angle reduces this danger. That is, a square edge on a stone will break more readily than a champfered edge, hence, strange as it seems, shallow cutting adds to the life expectancy of the incised letter.

The fundamental quality of Roman letters — as with all flat graphic statements — is contrast. One does not paint silver letters on an aluminum background nor black letters on slate. In chiselled letters the V-cut shadow, under ordinary conditions, is just not strong enough for easy reading of the inscription. It must be strengthened by the contrast of paint or gilding.

Figure 81 is a photo of a polyester cast of the Trajan Inscription. I made this casting of the original inscription in Rome for the Lakeside Press of the R. R. Donnelley Company of Chicago. The dark gray polyester was painted off-white to simulate the color of the Grecian marble in

Fig. 82. Paint and shadow in a section of the R. R. Donnelley polyester cast.

83

which the Roman letters are cut. The letters in the cast were then painted orange-siena to suggest the appearance of ancient Roman inscriptions in general and the Trajan Inscription in particular. Large, obvious breaks in the letters were left unpainted. It occurred to me while painting that this polyester cast could also be made into a witness against those who defend shadows in incised letters. Accordingly I omitted the paint from several letters of the first and second lines of the Inscription. These unpainted letters flanked by painted ones (Fig. 82) were then photographed outdoors in order to get deep and normal sun shadows. It is obvious which letters serve legibility better.

It should be reasonably clear, then, that the ancients gave no heed to cast shadows. It follows that the Roman calligrapher thought of letters, not as 3-dimensional, but as 2-dimensional, linear entities only. This point needs emphasis as we shall discover when we take up the primacy of the written shape among the Romans. One may say, then, that in essence the Roman inscription letter was linear although accidentally it has a V-cut, 3-dimensional existence.

14

Letter cutting in stone

efore going further, a brief description of stone letter-cutting is in order. In giving my own letter-cutting procedure, I am aware that it is not universal, that other methods exist, and that some authors and letter cutters disagree with me.

In 1931 when I first began letter cutting I had only books to instruct me. The tilted stone position that Eric Gill advised did not seem comfortable to me. It presented too many problems, was difficult to maneuver and less satisfactory for safety of worker and stone. As a sign writer I usually wrote on the flat or on a slightly tilted bench—about 20-25 degrees from the horizontal. It seemed natural to me that the same position should be used for writing and lettering on stone. After trying the slightly tilted position, I adopted the horizontal for its comfort and ease. Moreover, cutting on the flat permitted me to shift the stone around into any position and thus to get the benefit of the contrast provided by crosslights when chiselling the channel of V-cuts. In 1936 I was sure of the advantages of this position when I saw letterers in Greece, Italy, and Germany cutting on the flat.

Most English cutters seem to prefer the stone in the upright position, while the few American and European letterers I know prefer it flat. Each has advantages. I have cut on-the-job, vertical murals and inscriptions and find upright cutting more difficult and physically tiring. Then too, upright cutting often forces me to cut left-handed and since I prefer right-handed cutting this may color my preference for the flat. Perhaps it is a matter of what we are habituated to. Will Carter, the very fine English cutter, is firm in his view that upright cutting is easier. But, preferences aside, cutters should know both methods of cutting.

I suspect, although I am not sure, that Eric Gill's upright cutting determined the English letter-cutting stance. But many forget that Eric Gill was also a sculptor cutting figures in the 'round.' The stone is naturally fixed vertically so that the sculptor can walk around the figure while working on it, and also view it in the light and shadow of its normal, and final, vertical position. Gill became accustomed to working in this way and mounted all his lettering work upright, in like manner.

In cutting letters I find that I start with the stem, the letter's thickest element. The stem and stem-width largely determine proportions, establish the letter's vertical or slant orientation, and give the first, over-all approximation on spacing. The stems are the chief means for letter

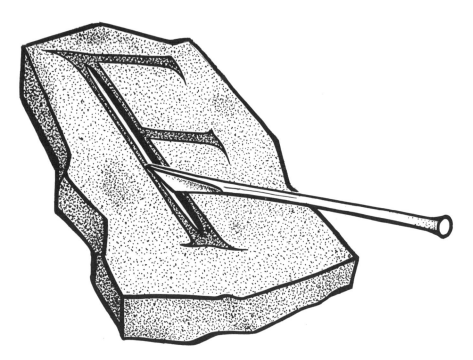

Fig. 83. Letter cutting in stone.

•

spacing and modifications of the letter to left or right can more easily be made with the thick stems. To begin, say, with the arm serifs of majuscule E would make impossible any change whatever in the width of that letter, whereas beginning in the center of E's stem would enable the cutter, while cutting from the inside out, to correct his spacing and proportioning if necessary.

This is especially true when cutting quick letters from informal, roughly sketched layouts. Of course the rule for cutting thick stems first is not without exception; there are times when one cuts the thin before the thick. For example, one would cut the cross bar to majuscule T first (as one does when writing the letter) for reasons of space composition.

I find that I start at the center of the letter-stem and chisel out towards the edge. The chisel, held at a constant cutting angle, alternates cuts on each side of the V-cut channel until the letter edge is *almost* reached. At this stage, thin strokes, arms, cross bars, and thin curves are cut and finished. The chisel is generally held at a steeper angle in cutting serifs, especially for the initial cut at the tip where one needs a quick and exact 'bite' with the chisel. I find that I always cut serifs from their tips into the stems and arms of letters. The serifs are blended into the fillets and into the outer edges of the letters, which *then are finished*. In making round shapes I start with the thick swells which are analogous to the thick stem.

Fig. 84. Photograph of V-cut ridging in stone.

87

I realize it is practically axiomatic to cut thins before thicks since cutting a thin arm into a finished stem would break out a part of the stem's V-cut wall at the juncture. The cutting method described above does not violate this axiom. The stem is begun before but not finished until after the serifs, fillets, bars, tails, and arms have been cut.

The distinctive and only contribution of the chisel is a tiny dentation or ridging caused by each mallet stroke on the V-cut sides. The harder the stone the finer is this herringbone or chevron striation. Light mallet taps cause smaller striations. In large outdoor letters (I have in mind some letters, 19″ tall, which I cut in Monson slate) there are about twenty-five ridges per inch. In small delicate lettering there would be more. This chisel texture is highly desirable since it catches and reflects light. It is particularly good under gold or palladium leaf.

Fig. 85. A questionable cutting method.

•

I never have occasion to make chisel cuts from the edge of the V-cut to its root with the chisel held parallel to the edge of the straight letter parts as shown in figure 85. However I know that Greek letterers in the

Classic and Hellenistic ages did use this method, but *only* for letters about one-half inch tall, that is, the width of the chisel. But the Greek cutter had a very special, and excellent, reason (a tract in itself) for employing this procedure, the explanation of which need not detain us here. I have seen Italian and French cutters using this method, indicated in figure 85, for larger letters but their letters were wretched. It presumes that stems, arms, cross bars, and obliques are mechanically straight, whereas, in the best letters, 'straight' parts instead have a delicate, hardly perceptible curvature. Anyone insensitive to this curvature in 'straight strokes would gravitate to the mechanical practice of figure 85. It is inappropriate since such a method cannot be used for round letters where instead one must adopt the V-cut ridging technique.

I know of no stone letterer who uses the V-shaped chisel (*veiner* or *parting tool*) to fashion the V-cuts of letters. I mention this because many readers unfamiliar with letter-cutting in stone but knowledgeable about the use of V-shaped chisels in wood carvings mistakenly assume that the V-shaped chisel also fashions the V-cut in stone-cut letters.

15

Cutting straight and curved letter parts

ome authors tell us that it is easier to cut straight than to cut curved letter shapes. In other words they think the chisel not only produced the serif but determined the overall "squarishness" of Roman capitals and the preference for straight letter-parts in which U, for example, appears as V.

●

V in Latin inscriptions stood normally for U as well as V, and is easier to cut in stone.

Frederic W. Goudy, *The Capitals from the Trajan Column in Rome,* p. 35.

●

Lapidary writing inscribed or incised with a chisel on stone, thus acquired a geometric quality, without curves or ligatures, in sharp contrast was the rapid writing permitted by the reed pen . . . or by the writing brush . . .

Encyclopedia of World Art (New York: McGraw Hill, 1960), III, 3.

●

The use of pen and ink on papyrus encouraged the making of curves, whereas chiselling on stone made for straight lines.

Aubry West, *Written by Hand* (London: George Allen & Unwin Ltd., 1935), p. 14.

●

In fact, however, the left oblique of V in fine, Imperial letters is a long, barely noticeable curve—and even the thick obliques in M and N

90

have this same delicate curvature. Furthermore the theory is upset by inspecting ancient Rustic capitals written and cut in stone, in which the

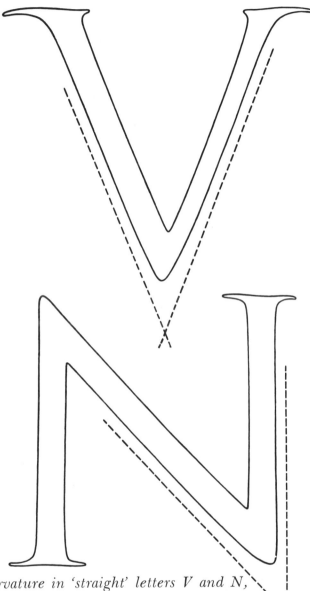

Fig. 86. Curvature in 'straight' letters V and N, taken from the first and third lines in the Trajan Inscription (3/5).

U's (Latin V) are rounded (Figs. 112, 114, 120.) Obviously it is easier to make a straight line with ruler or ruling pen than it is to make a free hand curve. It is also easier to judge the straightness of a line than the correctness of a curve. These factors may color the thinking of authors who write about, but have not cut, Roman letters.

I have already given some reasons why errors entered into our thinking about the origin of the serif. A suspicious corollary to the "stop"-mark theory for the origin of the serif here asserts itself. Those who say that the chisel prefers straight letter-parts over curves, and who also say that straight parts are easier to cut, may be thinking that the stone cutter does not cut with mallet strokes along the stem but that he cuts instead from the edge of the letter's stem to the root of the V-cut in the questionable manner described in figure 85, and that serifs are cut in much the same manner. With this kind of technique in mind it is not difficult to explain the genesis of authors' thinking that encourages them to say that straight letter parts are easier to cut.

The same authors who advance the chisel as the cause of the serif insist that the chisel determined the shapes of inscriptional Roman letters also.

●

These capitals are called square capitals from the rectangular nature of the junctions of strokes and the generally rectilinear formation which the chisel prefers.

Graily Hewitt, *Lettering*, p. 30.

●

. . . as it was easier to cut square capitals in stone . . .

Frederic W. Goudy, *The Alphabet and Elements of Lettering*, p. 42.

●

It is also possible that those who say that the chisel prefers straight elements may be influenced by the layman's graffito-attitude towards stone cutting. Graffiti or letter-scratching on durable materials is the

92

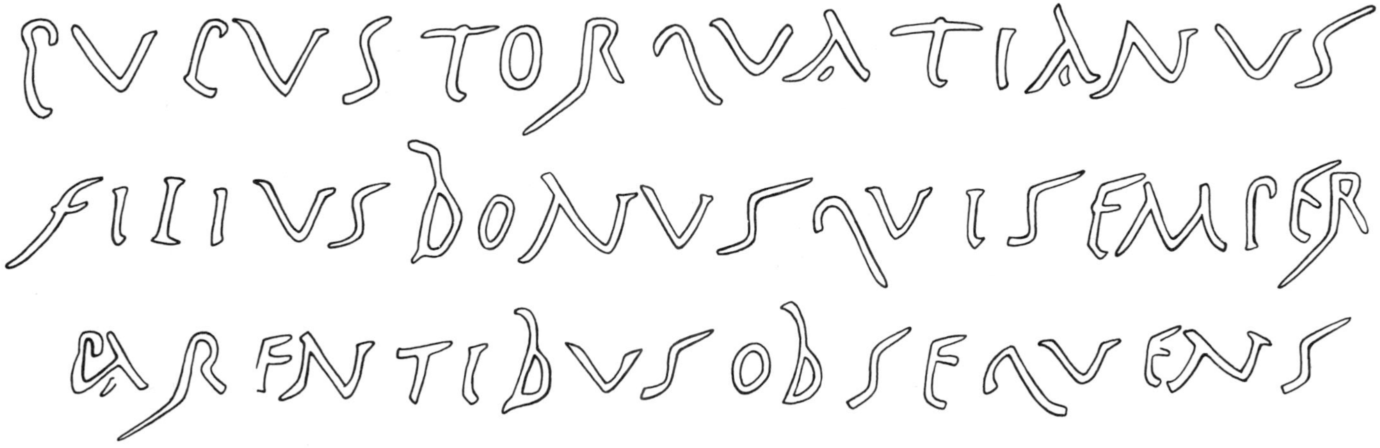

Fig. 87. Part of the third century sepulchral inscription of Pupus Tor-
quatianus written and cut in marble using cursive letters (1/2).
(PVPVSTORQVATIANVS— (2) FILIVSBONVSQVISEMPER –
(3) CARENTIBVSOBSEQVENS). Vatican Lapidary Galleries.

93

Fig. 88. Curves cut in stone (3/10).

amateur's attempt at calligraphy. Letters so made are composed mostly of straight and angular letter parts with practically no small or regularly shaped, consistent curves. The explanation is this: the amateur does not have his tools and materials under control. He uses unorthodox methods, often improper tools, which he forces with undue pressure to mark hard materials. Such scratchings made with uncontrolled force

Fig. 89. A third century Christian graffito.
St. John Lateran Museum, Rome.

•

will usually be straight or, on occasion, broadly curved and of unpredictable length, which explains as well why graffiti rise above and fall below top and bottom guide lines. On the other hand the professional letter cutter, after long practice and experience in using traditional techniques, has complete control of his tools, enabling him to cut any shape with the same delicacy of touch. He *never forces* his tools or ma-

95

terials. Consequently it is a matter of indifference to the competent inscription cutter whether a letter to be cut is round or straight (Cf. figs. 87, 88, and 102) excepting, of course, small, thin curves, whose radii are, say, less than a quarter of an inch.

The truth is, as any stone letterer will confirm, that it is no more difficult to cut curved than straight letter parts; and most cutters will agree that mistakes made in straight parts are more glaring than mistakes made in curved shapes. The chisel as a tool contributes nothing but the tiny striation of the V-cut, and in fine grained stones such as slate and lithographic limestone the *chisel can cut any shape* written by the brush. Indeed ancient Chinese letterers cut the delicately minute *dry brush streaks* made by their master calligraphers, as one can see by examining Langdon Warner's fine rubbings of Han Dynasty carvings from North China in Harvard's Fogg Museum archives.

16

Reed writing

The most significant characteristic in western calligraphy has been the shaded writing quality in written alphabet shapes. Faint foreshadowings or rudiments of this thick-and-thin, reed-writing character appeared earlier in Egyptian hieroglyphic, hieratic, and demotic writing. But the credit for the use of the sharp, square-edged writing tool as a major calligraphic design element belongs

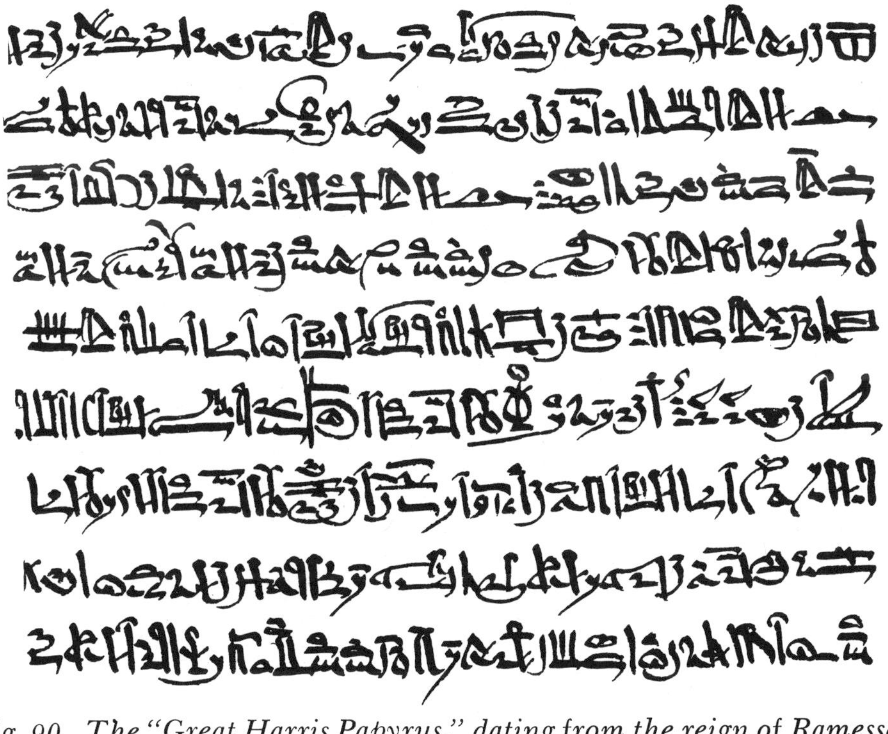

Fig. 90. The "Great Harris Papyrus," dating from the reign of Ramesses IVth (c. 1166-1160 B.C.) Reproduced by permission of the Trustees of the British Museum.

to the Romans. The Romans inherited the sans-serif, stilus alphabet from the Etruscans who in turn were indebted to the Aeolic-Chalcidian Greeks. One can say that the Roman alphabet, with slight modifications and changes, owes it mental images to its Etruscan origins, and the technical development of these to the square-edged reed.

The Phoenicians had used the reed as a stilus on clay as early as 3100 B.C., for clay and reed were plentiful in southern Babylonia. Earlier still the Egyptians wrote with the rush, *Juncus Maritimus,* the end of which was cut at a slant and its fibers split by chewing to produce a small chisel-shaped 'brush.' The Greeks used a reed-pen made from *Phragmites Aegyptiaca.* The reeds *Arundo Donas* and *Phragmites Communis* were common in Mediterranean countries.

In addition, papyrologists tell us that papyrus was the chief writing material for book production in Greece from at least the seventh century B.C., and that the method of preserving and circulating literature in early Rome did not differ from that of Greece. Papyrus was used for public and private letters, receipts, accounts, contracts, birth notices, etc. We know that a great national literature devoted to tragedies, comedies, poems, satires, epigrams, histories, and epics was developing in Rome in the second half of the third and in the second century B.C. Literary historians tell us that Latin literature, based on Greek models, begins with the end of the First Punic War (241 B.C.)

When did the Roman thick-and-thin development take place? Until more exact information is forthcoming I would place the Roman adoption of the reed-written alphabet in the second century B.C., since all the pre-requisite conditions, materials, authors, and their publishing needs were present. David Diringer points out in *The Hand Produced Book,* p. 556, that ". . . the reed-pen was used, for writing on papyrus, at least from the third century B.C. onwards; it was called in Greek *kálamos,* and Latin *calamus* . . . and the exact term for reed-pen was *calamus scriptorius* or *chartarius* (i.e., papyrus)."

Using the square-edged reed as a writing tool there are many possibilities for alphabet design. A look at Celtic, Chancery, Square Capitals, and Rustic letter-making shows some of these possibilities. Each of

98

these hands differs in its cant; for example, Celtic has almost zero degrees cant and Rustic about 70-80 degrees.

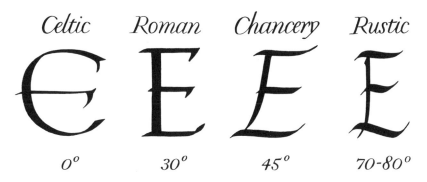

Fig. 91. Cant variations in some historical bookhands.

•

The Roman scribe made a unique contribution in the cant he adopted. With the many cant angles from which to choose, the Roman scribe selected that angle (25-30 degrees) which produces a normal horizontal stroke one-half as thick as the vertical stroke. This choice gave us the pleasing alternation of thick and thin in the Roman alphabet — the 2 : 1 proportion that has been its basic, identifying trait ever since.

Fig. 92. Basic, 2 : 1, vertical-horizontal, stroke-width proportions characteristic of the Roman alphabet.

•

One could ask why the Roman reed writer did not write with zero degrees cant to fashion letters with thin horizontals as in late Half-Uncial writing, which, stylistically and technically, is easier to write? The answer is simply that the thin horizontal mark made by the reed in Half-

Uncial letters is too unlike the thick vertical. Such a thin horizontal stroke is visually weak, therefore an impediment to legibility.

While we may admire Irish Half-Uncial letters with zero degrees cant, the fact remains that, of the many reed-pen possibilities, letters with 25-30 degrees cant are the most legible. In proof, Insular calligraphers (e.g., in the Book of Kells), found it necessary to fatten the

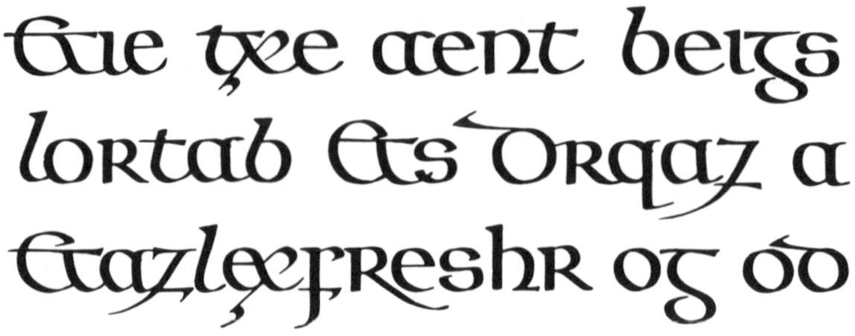

Ħıe ŧꝛe ꝏent beıꞇs lortab Ħs‘Orqaz a Ħꞇazlæfꞃeshꞃ oꞇ óo

Fig. 93. Half-Uncial writing.

•

ends of weak horizontals as did the calligraphers who produced Square Capitals in the third and fourth centuries A.D. In the strictest sense Uncial, Half-Uncial, and Square Capitals are not writing throughout.

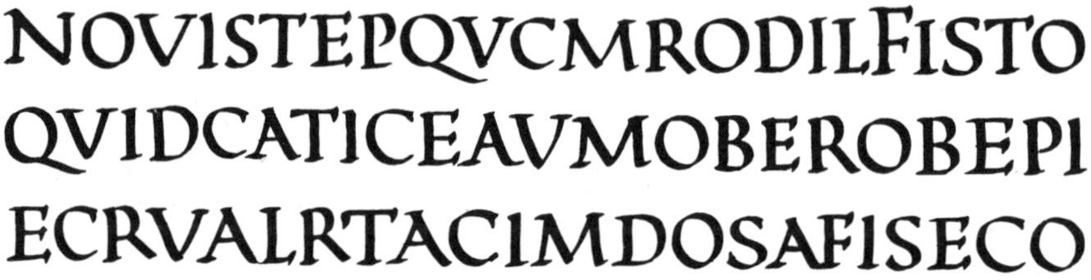

NOVISTEPQVCMRODILFISTO QVIDCATICEAVMOBEROBEPI ECRVALRTACIMDOSAFISECO

Fig. 94. Square Capitals bookhand.

•

The thin horizontals common to these hands were often built-up and filled-in, therefore partly in the realm of lettering. We could call these hands 'writing-lettering' (in which some needed strokes or letter parts are usually written in two strokes rather than in one) in the same sense we call Versals and present day sign-writer's bold, block letters (Cf. p. 277 and figures 233 and 234) types of writing-lettering, that is, following a more or less predictable stroke sequence and stroke direction.

100

One could venture the statement that, of the many choices, the Roman cant selection of 25-30 degrees is the best. Rustic writing with its great cant of 70-80 degrees was, for a time, calligraphically, stylistically, and, perhaps even economically, acceptable; but its decline after a few

BRVTPAPIRVQVTVSPQVIDI
SPQVRVESTLVAVMVISIQIR

Fig. 95. Rustic writing.

•

centuries of use suggests that it was too extreme. The functional value of Celtic writing, as indicated before, with near-zero cant, is debatable and writing with 45 degrees cant, so popular among calligraphers today, has some inherent disadvantages.

ELTAXEHVLETAVLL
eolit caen fourit xol

Fig. 96. Writing with 45 degrees cant.

•

EPIGRYAFDHKELI
orit caent hior Egrdi

Fig. 97. Writing with 30 degrees cant.

101

Just as we have patterns of auditory expectancy so we have visual. Trite sayings such as "atheistic Communism," "decadent capitalism," "rugged individualism," go "hand in hand" and are "tried and true." We call these hackneyed expressions. We hear the first word and from habitual iteration we expect and often supply its mate. Fortunately, in time, such phrases lose their usefulness and are supplanted. In contrast we acquire visual habits and patterns of expectancy but, unlike auditory clichés, they are not ordinarily supplanted. Indeed our visual patterns of expectancy border on immutability, neighbor to universal law.

Speaking generally we tend to expect important parallels to be vertical rather than horizontal. We see about us trees, and houses, people walking and standing, things which must achieve at least some degree of verticality to remain what they are. We associate living, dynamic qualities with the vertical while the horizontal is more suggestive of non-living and static states. Thus it is that we react to verticals more than to horizontals and this visual habit plus the ever-present experience of gravity combine to form within us a convincing *pattern of expectancy*. It is a familiar fact that, in writing vertically symmetrical letters such as B, C, D, E, H, K, N, O, S, X, and Z, their upper parts must be made smaller so that they will appear equal to the lower part which otherwise they would overwhelm.

As another example, the true square looks dumpy because of this optical downward thrust of its top and sides. A square looks square only

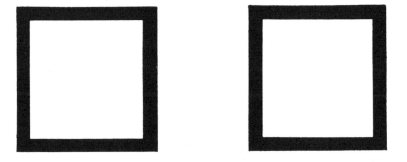

Fig. 98. A true square and an optically compensated 'square'.

when it is taller than it is wide. Thus it is that our patterns of visual expectancy demand that verticals be made stouter and longer than horizontals. This is the reason majuscules E, F, H, L, Z and numerals 2, 5, and 7 must have shorter horizontal arms than their vertical stems and

ETPH

Fig. 99. Sans-serif letters with thicker verticals than horizontals.

heights. A horizontal arm equal in thickness and length to its vertical stem will be optically thicker and longer. Even well designed sans-serif letters will have their horizontals ever so slightly thinner than their vertical parts so that all parts *will appear equal* optically.

Fig.100. "Writings" at zero, 30 and 45 degrees cant.

103

In letter-making there should be a balanced relationship among all the parts. Roman letter parts may be reduced ultimately to three sorts: vertical, horizontal and oblique; with three corresponding sorts of curves. Accordingly when writing the elements at zero, 30, and 45 degrees cant, the stroke relationships in figure 100 occur. Some readers may object to these serifless pseudo-letters. In any analysis one strips away non-essentials in order to arrive at the subject's essence. Serifs, because they are accidentals, can interfere with the raw appraisal of the legibility-factor possessed by these 'letters' of varying cants. For this reason serifs are omitted and pseudo-letters in place of actual letters are mostly used in figure 100.

It is clear that writing at zero and 70-80 degrees cant fashions a thin

Fig. 101. Some cant expressions from the past at 30°, 0°, 45°, 70-80° and 0°

104

stroke which differs too much from the thick one, and, because of its thinness, is difficult to read. It is clear also that writing at 45 degrees cant produces mechanically equal horizontal and vertical strokes which, however, are *optically unequal*. These two factors — vertical-horizontal pattern of expectation and thick-thin relationship — are most satisfactorily balanced in Roman letters of 30 degrees cant. The fact that this 2 : 1 proportion has endured over the centuries is a pragmatic argument for its reasonableness.

17

Pen or chisel first?

The exaggerated respect for stone-cut letters as such, which we have seen associated with the 'clean marble' idea, tends to support the notion that letter cutting came before letter writing.

Many authors, for example, Hans Meyer *(The Development of writing)*, Oscar Ogg *(An Alphabet Source Book)*, Percy Smith *(Lettering and Writing)*, show 'evolutionary trees' or diagrams in which all western letters, Square Capitals, Rustic, Cursive Majuscule-minuscules, Insular, Gothic, Merovingian, Carolingian, etc. are derived from one source—the Roman lapidary models.

●

The first Roman scripts, were, like the Greek ones, carved in stone.

Hans Meyer, *The Development of Writing* (Zurich: Amstutz & Herdig, 1961), p. 8.

●

The early Roman scribe based his written forms on stone-cut letters . . .

Frederic W. Goudy, *The Alphabet and Elements of Lettering*, p. 48.

●

Die Quadrata versucht, die Kapitalschrift und ihre meisselbedingten Formen durch staendige Federdrehung nachzunehmen.

Albert Kapr, *Deutsche Schriftkunst* (Dresden: Verlag der Kunst, 1959), p. 20.

●

●

When stone and chisel are discarded for papyrus and reed-pen . . .
the Latin alphabet first appears in the epigraphic type . . . These characters form the main stem from which developed all the branches of Latin
writing.

Encyclopaedia Britannica, 1965, XVII, 98.

●

If we admit, as it seems we must admit, that in Roman times the
public inscription in stone was the chief model for all forms of letters,
we shall expect to find that when they began to make letters with a pen,
on paper or skin, the forms of letters would be imitations of inscription
forms, and this is precisely what we do find.

Eric Gill, *An Essay on Typography* (London: Sheed & Ward, 1931),
p. 28.

●

These are extremely important characteristics which seem to derive
from the tool — actually more probably from the chisel than the pen, as
one often sees stated; they come as naturally to the chisel, and are found
much earlier in carvings than in script.

Nicolete Gray, *Lettering on Buildings,* p. 21.

●

Preceding either [square and pointed pens] was no doubt a tool for
scratching or cutting stone or bone, which became the chisel with which
the magnificent Greek and Roman inscriptions were executed.

Graily Hewitt, *Lettering,* p. 26.

●

The manipulation of the chisel in stone caused the element known
as the *serif* to come to be. Since such an ending is a natural, rational
thinking, the serif became an integral part of the letter form. It has logi-
cally carried over into later pen-drawn descendants.

Oscar Ogg, *An Alphabet Source Book,* p. 35.

●

107

It is more reasonable to believe that writing and cutting letters in durable materials appears in a culture when standardized shapes have been accepted by the reading public after letter-writing practice and experimentation on softer, more tractable materials such as clay, bark, leaves, linen, skins, and wax.

Soft materials were used for recording permanent writings in the early days of Greece and Rome. Pliny (H.N. xiii, 69) states that Homer knew of the existence of wood-tablet (wax- or gesso-lined) books before the age of Troy. *Pugillarium enim usum fuisse etiam ante Troiana tempora invenimus apud Homerum.* Livy (x, 38) mentions the use of linen by the Samnites who 'in that place offered sacrifice following directions read from an old linen roll, the celebrant being the aged Ovius Paccius who said he derived the ceremony from an ancient Samnite ritual.' *Ibi ex libro vetere linteo . . . sacerdote Ovio Paccio . . . qui se id sacrum petere adfirmabat ex vetusta Samnitium religione . . .* (B.C. 293). The Sibylline Books bought by Lucius Tarquinius Superbus (534-510 B.C.) are generally considered to have been linen books and David Diringer tells us that ". . . linen seems to have been the substance on which sacred books and ancient records of Rome were written." David Diringer, *The Hand-Written Book,* p. 45.

It is inconceivable that the first letter shapes were chisel-cut in stone, then copied in other materials. The fact that we have no Roman writing on softer material such as papyrus, leaves, skins, wood, and cloth before the first century B.C., and innumerable inscriptions in hard materials from centuries before should not mislead us into believing that the one came from the other. There are many Egyptian papyrii dating back to the third millenium B.C., it is true, but Egypt has a climate favorable to the preservation of delicate, soft writing materials, while Rome has not. The vestiges of Rome's vulnerable writing have perished.

The survival of letters in hard materials is not the only reason for this belief. Another is the natural tendency for authors and typographers to be interested in fine calligraphic examples and to ignore ordinary, everyday writing. This in turn has led to some doubtful trains of

108

thought, such as the unwarranted canonization of glyptic shapes because of their beauty and historic interest at the expense of ordinary, informal cursives, and to the conclusion that inscriptional shapes were the model and inspiration for subsequent writing and lettering.

We have stone-cut Uncial letters. Hübner states that Uncial was *first* a bookhand[6] and was only later cut in stone[7]. I am convinced that the Imperial inscriptional alphabet is the refined lettering offshoot of the letters in which books were written which in turn were part of the vital stream of everyday writing, that is *scriptura communis.* "For scripts, like populations," as Dr. E. A. Lowe of the Institute for Advanced Study remarks, "recruit chiefly from below."[8]

18

Writing & lettering

Fictions that Roman writing copied stone models (lettering) has tended to blind us to important truths about writing and lettering. Ordinarily we tend to value lettering above writing by reason of the general truth that it is easier to understand the *accidental* marks of anything than it is to grasp its *essential* traits.

Now the accidental consists of data perceived by the senses. The essential, because it stems from the mind, tends to the abstract, away from localization in sense and is, therefore, more difficult to grasp and appraise than sense experience.

Accidentals are such things as size, cost, purpose, scarcity, authorship, durability, preciousness, position, material, effort, etc. Given two examples of letter production of equal merit, that possessing more accidental marks would generally be more highly prized.

For example, because stone cutting today is rare an inscription cut in stone would be preferred to one written on paper though the two were equally skillful and beautiful.

But suppose that stone inscriptions were being made and used as frequently as neon tube signs or gold leaf window lettering. Would we think so highly of stone cut lettering? Hardly. We would probably regard all of them in about the same light.

But in the art of calligraphy, as in all arts, the idea in the mind is the ultimate yardstick by which we evaluate merit in the art-product. The technical pre-requisites — tools, materials, and method of working — though needed, are always subordinate to their mental exemplar. Technique is only a means. Skillfully wrought expressions of inconsequential ideas are more likely to arouse dismay than admiration. Poorly written letters skillfully chiselled are always uglier than well-written letters poorly cut since a defect in the means is less damaging than a defect in the mental pattern.

Writing is the internal and external basis for lettering, for, according to our definition, lettering is the multi-stroked expansion of writing, hence lettering comes after, not before its parent.

Externalization of the mental pattern is the end-product of art. This external statement is wholly dependent on the internally conceived "word." It is difficult for us in the western world to appreciate to what extent our cultural tendencies in the graphic arts lean to lettering-drawing rather than writing-drawing. Lettering does not have the closeness to its formal origins that writing has. Writing is the direct and immediate link to the formal concept in the mind of the artist, whereas lettering is, in a manner of speaking, worked-over or "improved" writing.

In the past several centuries we Westerners have acquired a high regard for typographic and related graphic expressions. We overlook, however, the fact that typefaces (lettering) owe their formal existence to writing, and that type is, in fact, the 'frozen handwriting' of the early Humanists. We are far removed from the Chinese ideal in the letter-making arts. It would be unthinkable to a Chinese calligrapher, for example, to make a planned, preliminary drawing on silk before painting. After long, contemplative immersion he begets his "word." When he considers the moment ripe he writes directly, with no preliminary sketching, the inwardly conceived "word" into the calligraphy we see. And having written his art-product he deems it finished. He does not try to "improve" it by retracing over strokes, deleting, or retouching.

Our western culture in graphic arts on the other hand is more sympathetic to drawing as a preliminary step to painting, as well as to touching up and improving. This indicates in part our western appreciation of lettering and our seeming neglect of writing. It explains partly our inability to appraise correctly the writing foundation to Imperial calligraphy. It would appear that the Romans, not burdened with our 500-years-old experience of typography and lettering, were in what we think of as the Eastern tradition, which appreciates the primacy and

111

immediacy of writing.

At this point some reader might ask: what about the resemblance between Square Capitals, say, and inscription letters; and, is it not true that Square Capitals were copied from stone-cut letters? Before answering we should understand a thing or two about the names "Square Capitals" and 'Square Letters.'

In the first century B.C. Marcus Vitruvius, the Roman engineer-architect who wrote the famous book on architecture, stated the geometric and numerical canon that 'man's anatomical proportions are reducible to the ratio 1 to 10, the circle, and square.' In the Renaissance, Felice Feliciano, one of the first 'circle-and-square' calligraphers who influenced subsequent letter design, extended this Vitruvian canon *homo ad quadratum et ad circulum* to capital roman letters. It may be that *littera quadrata* in part was derived from Feliciano's canon that letters are based on the square and circle — *littera ad quadratum et ad circulum*. The geometry-theory of calligraphy has numerous defenders in our time. For example, we read that '. . . the square and the circle, . . . are undoubtedly the basis of the square capital, . . .' (Nicolete Gray, *Lettering on Buildings,* p. 21), and L'Harl Copeland contends that the Romans arrived at their "harmonious alphabet of 24 letters" through the use of a formula involving the circle, square and half-squares, that is, two smaller squares in vertical position. (L'Harl Copeland, *Design of the Roman Letters* New York: Philosophical Library, 1966).

Moreover at about the turn of the last century the term *litterae quadratae*[9] was mistranslated into "Square Letters," suggesting the notions that monumental letters are square[10], and that pen-made letters, supposedly copied from them should be called "Square Letters." The adjective *quadrata* in this context does not mean *square* but means having to do with the mason's *job* of *squaring stones,* that is, shaping them. "Stone mason's letters" would be a proper translation, or "monumental," "stone-cut," "glyptic," or simply "inscriptional letters." We cannot say just when, and by whom, this mistranslation was popularized. In 1885, when Emil Hübner wrote his *Exempla Scripturae Epigraphicae Latinae,* the correct version was still accepted, at least by

112

him. ". . . *nequaquam igitur a forma quadratae litterae nomen ac-ceperunt*," page xxvi; "It is by no means from their shapes, therefore, that *'litterae quadratae'* took their name," wrote Hübner. Another inference, often repeated, would have us believe that 'these letters are called Square Capitals because most of the letters fit within a square.' *"Der Name [Quadrata] enstand, weil die meisten Buchstaben einem Quadrat enstehen."* Albert Kapr, *Deutsche Schriftkunst* (Dresden: Verlag der Kunst, 1959), p. 21.

A still further confusion arose when it was assumed that the "Square Capitals"[11] of the Latin bookhand were derived from the "Square Capitals" cut in stone.[12] There seems to be no basis for this assumption. On the contrary it is disproved by the use of thin strokes in the bookhand which do not occur in the monumental letters. One does not need to know much about the writing tool to see that the thin strokes in the bookhand are the direct result of the reed held at a characteristic angle and manipulated in its own special manner.

Nor are the serifs that terminate these thin strokes in the bookhand copied from stone-cut letters. They are of quite a different character. With a cant of not much more than zero degrees, the book scribes of the "Square Capitals" found that their thin horizontal strokes needed the emphasis of a terminal serif if they were to be fully legible. This same need for accenting the poorly visible horizontals led the Irish who wrote Half-Uncials with zero degrees cant to the same solution.

The terminal arm serif of the stone-cut E results from a flick of the writing brush held at a cant of about 30 degrees. This cant gives a horizontal stroke strong enough to be visible even without the serif, but the ink- or pigment-filled brush must leave the stone surface somehow, and this twist of the wrist, finger roll, and twirl of the brush is the traditional Roman way of doing it. And very beautiful it is, if one has skill enough to produce it (Cf. figs. 175, 176, and 177, pages 177 f.) The book writing scribe, on the other hand, using a different tool, held at a different angle, and for a different purpose, produced a different serif.

It seems more reasonable to think that Square Capitals were developed in an attempt to return to more slowly made letter shapes and

113

to counteract the informal, minusculizing tendencies at work in the vast amount of rapid writing done at that time. Each writing reform is generally away from informality towards formality. Square Capitals are more formal, carefully made and slowly made, with each letter part distinct and characteristically consistent, than are the cursive, majuscule-mixed-minuscule letters of that time.

We have too many examples of stone-cut letters looking exactly like semi-formal and informal brush writing to believe those who hold that the scribe in writing books imitated lettered inscription shapes.

Unlike the Romans and Chinese we Westerners are more impersonal in our approach to letters. The standardization of our alphabet since the invention of printing accounts in part for our tendency to value the external appearance of letters above individual calligraphic expression. Today we seem to esteem ancient inscriptions which coincide with our alphabetic norms and to dismiss informal and rudely cut inscriptions which do not. We even assume that the incising of informal writings was the work of unskilled cutters. It is true the Romans had

Fig. 102. Third century cursive capitals skillfully cut in marble. Vatican Lapidary Galleries. Full size.

•

but one alphabet; nevertheless, it was written, and even cut in stone, with wide variations of formality and informality. Important civic pro-

114

nouncements most often were laid out and cut with great care. But for unofficial purposes writing that was cramped, ligatured, freely abbreviated, mis-spaced and laid out without guide lines prior to cutting, appears to have been acceptable as long as it could be read. Such unskilled writing may even have had on occasion value as the direct expression of its scribe.

Figure 103 shows some ligatures taken from the Dacian Wax Tablets written in the second century. If one compares these letters with other capitals written in the same century, say, figures 104 through 124,

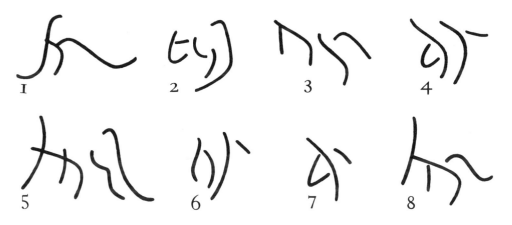

Fig. 103. Second century ligatures taken out of context. The letters are: 1) FR; 2) EGI; 3) HA; 4) DAR; 5) HAB; 6) PAR; 7) TRI; 8) HA.

•

he can see how broad the band of letter-acceptance was in the late Republic and the Empire. Some of these Dacian ligatures, removed from their context, could prove a bit puzzling even to the trained paleographer.

There are many examples indicating the esteem Romans had for the primacy of writing and their seeming disregard of the importance of chiselling in the inscription sequence. For example, the two more common methods for laying out inscriptions was by massing the text like a newspaper column or centering the text as on a title page. It

115

seems that ancient sign writers like present day writers on occasion underestimated the amount of space needed for a line of writing. Thus in centered layouts this accounts for lines overbalanced to the right, and, in massed arrangements, for cramped and ligatured letters at the ends of lines. Even the Trajan Inscription has a hint of this free-writing method of letter-composition as one can note by comparing the open spacing of the letters at the end of the sixth line and the closed spacing of the third, fourth and fifth line endings with the spacing given to letters at the beginnings of these lines.

TAMENTO
RELICTIESSEN

Fig. 104. Part of a first century inscription with normal spacing followed by a line whose right end contains cramped and ligatured letters (1/2). Naples, National Museum.

•

In the National Museum of Naples there is an inscription from Herculaneum in excellent monumental letters in which the final T of the word RESTVIT has only the left arm. The right arm of this T was omitted because the sign writer ran short of space (Cf. Hübner, no. 331). Also in the Naples Museum there is a Caesarian inscription from the first century B.C. whose last line reads TESTAMENTO. The sign writer was too generous in spacing the letters of the fore part of this line. As a result he had practically no space left for the final T and O. To fit in these two letters he extended the right stem of N upwards across the top of which he placed T's arm. He made letter O less than one-quarter of its normal height, which he then squeezed against the stem of N

116

(Fig. 105). In the Vatican Museum there is an Augustan inscription in which N's last stem (of the word STRATONICE) extends below the line, to act as the letter I, and the E is written, quite small, inside the

Fig. 105. Part of a line from an inscription in the Naples National Museum with letters ligatured and compressed to fit the stone; second half of first century B.C. (1/2).

•

letter C. Figures 106 through 110 show lines from five different inscriptions with terminal letters ligatured and squeezed in order to fit their stones.

Our western lettering mentality reacts against these awkward dislocations. We appraise the chiselling (lettering) as more important and accordingly we, confronted with a like situation, would have sponged away (erased) the writing in order to respace the inscription. We can also infer from this Roman inscription practice that ancient letter cutters were very fast for, had letter cutters been slow, one certainly would think that the quick part of any process would be redone as a concession to the slow, tedious part of that process.

The principle of causality gives a final argument for the priority of writing over lettering. That is, the idea of the thing made must first be in the mind of the maker. Any part presumes its whole. Making any part of a letter by built-up, filled-in, and chisel techniques presupposes a concept of the whole letter. But the concept of the letter parts and their relative proportions and relationships to the whole letter is de-

117

rived from that method which externalizes the concept in its entirety; that is, by writing. Summing up, writing came first and inscription carving (lettering) followed. Figures 104 through 124 are Roman stone-cut inscriptions from the first centuries. They are inserted here to show their brush writing origins.

Our material for the past 58 pages has covered the chiselled V-cut, shadows in inscription letters, letter-cutting in stone, straight and curved letter parts, the primacy of writing, our western lettering mentality, the antecedence of plebian scripts over epigraphic productions, Rome's reed-writing invention, *litterae quadratae,* and historic cant-expression. This broad assemblage of material may strike the reader as no more than a series of disconnected, though interesting, digressions from our central serif theme. Actually, the conclusions just presented are vital. They provide background material necessary for what comes next.

118

Fig. 106, 107, 108, 109, 110. Five unrelated, first century inscriptions, three from the Naples National Museum and two from the Vatican Lapidary Galleries, showing ligatures and compressions made by ancient sign writers in order to keep lines within the right border of stones.

119

Fig. 111. Sabina, Wife of the Emperor Hadrian, (117-138 A.D.) Carthage Museum, Africa, (1/3).

VALERI·T
NERVAE·TRAIANI·AVG·GERM·AN

Fig. 112. National Museum, Rome, 105 A.D.

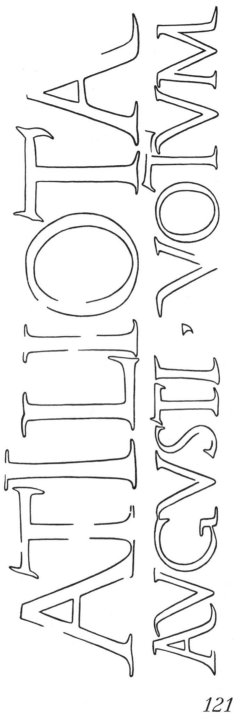

ATILIOTA
AVGVSTI · VOIVM
AVGVSII · VOIVM

Fig. 113. Narbonne Museum, France, 11 A.D.

121

Fig. 114. Third century, American Academy, Rome.

·

POSTVMI·MODE

M·SALA'R

Fig. 115. First century inscription from
Pompeii. Naples, National Museum.

·

E G·VIR

IMP·XS

Fig. 116. First century. Naples, National Museum.

122

Fig. 117. Inscription from Puteoli eulogizing Emperor Vespasian, ca. 92 A.D. Naples, National Museum.

Fig. 118. First century. Forum of Augustus, Rome. (2/5).

TARQVINIENS

Fig. 119. Oration of Claudius
to the Senate. Bronze (reed writing in wax). Lyons Museum, France, 46 A.D.

CLAVDII·GERMA
N(·)NAS · IANVAR

Fig. 120. Claudian dedication, 59-60. National Museum, Rome.

EPS·V·RBAI

Fig. 121. Dedication to Emperor Claudius. Palazzo del Drago. Rome. (1/3).

Fig. 122. *Third century epitaph, American Academy of Rome.* (½).

125

Fig. 123. *First century Pompeian inscription, Naples, National Museum. (2/3).*

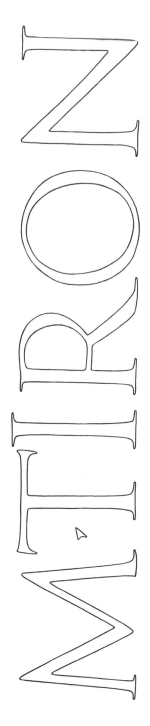

Fig. 124. *First century inscription, Ravenna, National Museum (1/3).*

19

Reed writing & practice

istorically the square-edged reed is Rome's distinctive writing tool. Lacking the reed, the shaded, thick-and-thin, "Roman" trait would never have entered the Latin alphabet. Though the reed is not the serif-solution we seek, it is, nevertheless, an important stepping stone to the key solution. At this point we need to understand reed manipulation and its basic kinetics.

A fundamental factor in shaded writing is its cant angle. Once this angle is fixed it generally does not change for a body of writing except

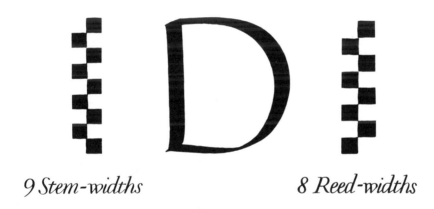

9 *Stem-widths*   8 *Reed-widths*

Fig. 125. Stem- and reed-width to letter-height proportions
in normal thick-and-thin Roman letters.

•

for special effects. The smaller the writing the fewer opportunities there are for varying cant. Even in large writing, cant will vary little if the reed-width is abnormally broad in relation to letter-height. Capitals

127

in normal shaded writing (Fig. 126) and in monumental capitals as well, are from eight to ten stem-widths tall. Conversely, when reed-width is very narrow in relation to letter-height, or when the writing edge of the reed has become blunted or rounded, variations in cant angle are not so noticeable.

1:13   1:9   1:6

Fig. 126. Thin, normal, and thick stem-to-height proportions.

•

Right-handed calligraphers writing Roman letters with the reed find certain strokes habitually recurring. The head serif in diagram *a* of figure 127 is not consciously sought. It soon becomes a part of every

a.   *b.*   *c.*

Fig. 127. Reed strokes.

•

stem for it is no more than a short movement along the thin edge of the reed to start the ink flowing, for the ink dries quickly on the reed edge.

128

Experience soon teaches the reed writer that if he attempts making stem strokes without this short, initial wiggle along the thin edge, the upper parts of his strokes will be frayed, gray, short of ink, uneven and often showing the slit of the reed nib as in diagrams *b* and *c.*

Ink is fed from the ink retainer down the slit of the reed to the reed tip and, in order to get an even distribution of ink along the entire writing edge of the reed, the initial wiggle is needed. The foot serif in diagram *a* is the answer to several problems. Beginners usually end stems without the serif as in diagram *b* and *c* — and the wise teacher suggests this in the beginning. But when stopping at the bottom of the stem the beginner discovers that excess ink has accumulated there. The reason is that the ink, flowing from the retainer along the nib-slit to reed edge, acquires a rapid flow-momentum as the reed makes its strokes from

Fig. 128. "Thin" writing.

•

top to bottom. This flow-momentum continues during the slowing down of the stroke as it approaches the bottom of the stem. The result is that when the reed halts more ink is deposited than is needed (diagram *c*) causing blobbed, rounded bottoms, delaying drying time, and adding to the danger of smearing the wet stroke. With skill the writer learns that he can decrease the amount of ink left at the foot by ending the stroke abruptly and by making immediately a sharp, quick flick to the right — and is thus enabled to write more letters with each ink re-filling as well.

This little wiggle at the top of vertical strokes and the corresponding flick to the right at the bottom are not only valid but, as we shall see in a moment, most important uses of the thinnest strokes that a well-cut

129

reed can make. Here the designation 'thick and thin' needs amending. 'Thick' may mean the thickest but 'thin' docs not mean thinnest. As mentioned earlier the square-edged reed held at the usual Roman cant angle produces shaded writing having verticals about twice as wide as horizontal letter parts — that is the 2 : 1 proportion characteristic of Roman letters. Well-made shaded writing utilizes the thickest strokes of the reed but not the easier-to-make thinnest, or edge stroke of the reed. When this thinnest, or minimal hairline, is used as a letter part, such parts are too thin to be fully legible, and hence mean that the reader has to guess.

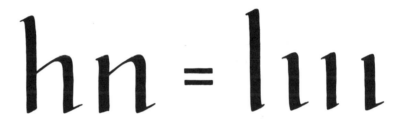

Fig. 129. Letters "hn" misread as other letters.

•

For example, lower case *e* made with the thinnest edge stroke is easily misread as *c,* and *h, m, n, u,* etc., may be mistaken for other letters. The combination *hn,* made with hairline thins, looks like *lin, lni, hii,* or *hu.* A chief complaint against Old English and Gothic scripts is the

mimaceous mimic

Fig. 130. Hairlines impede legibility in Old English letters.

•

confusion caused by almost invisible hairlines used as distinctive letter parts (Fig. 130).

There are several ways of reducing the illegibility of hairlines out

130

of place. 1) The thin strokes of letters may be strengthened by a slight change of direction, by not allowing the writing tool to course along its thinnest edge. 2) The bows at the upper right and lower left of such letters as *o, c, e, d,* etc., can be flattened. This flat curve is easy to make,

Fig. 131. Flattened bows in reed-made letters.

•

gives sharp internal angles, and lemon-shaped counters to round letters which aid legibility. 3) There is what we call "push-stroking," (Cf. figs. 7 and 132) by which the number of strokes is reduced, and in certain

Fig. 132. Push-stroking.

•

situations the reed is pushed instead of pulled. For example, S may thus be written in one stroke instead of two or three. This is a difficult skill to learn for it requires a light though firmly controlled touch, without which the letters tend to degenerate into informal cursives. Push-stroking helps the accomplished calligrapher to avoid the thinnest edge of the reed. It also saves time, as the tool is not lifted between strokes for changes of direction, and it fashions those crisp, internal angles mentioned which are so characteristic of the best monumental letters, especially B, and R.

But, despite the omission of the thinnest reed-mark (edge stroke)

131

from letter parts, every stroke begins and ends with a slight coursing along the reed edge fashioning a small, left head-serif and right foot-serif.

After much letter shaping experience one of the last skills the reed writing calligrapher learns is the reed twirl at the right end of the arms of C, E, F, G, L, S, and T. It is made by rotating the reed on the left

Fig. 133. Reed twirling fashioning right arm-serifs.

corner of its writing edge, then drawing the wet ink along in a continuation of the arm's inner curve, or along the edge of straight arms and stems. This and related finish strokes were commonplace in Roman literary hands, and later Uncial, Insular, Caroline, etc., scripts, and their

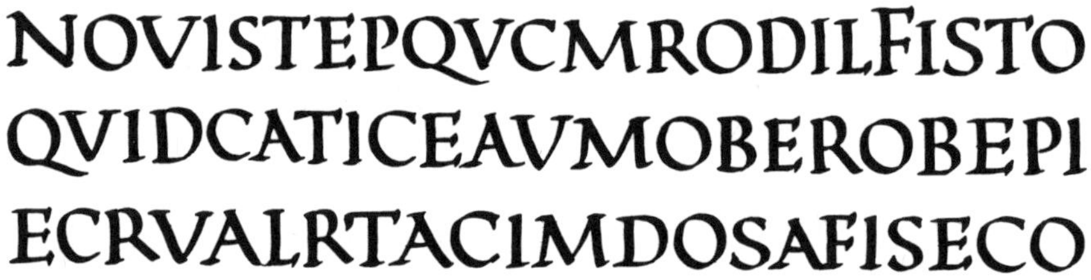

NOVISTEPQVCMRODILFISTO
QVIDCATICEAVMOBEROBEPI
ECRVALRTACIMDOSAFISECO

Fig. 134. Reed twirled endings in Square Capitals.

purpose was to get a somewhat neater arm ending than that normally made by the canted reed or quill pen.

132

But head and foot-serifs — made naturally by the reed and necessary to reed writing — might lead one to think that inscription serifs are derived from the reed-pen. Close inspection of inscriptional serifs and comparison of them with reed serifs, however, shows the inference to be false. A case could be made from the near resemblance between the right arm-serifs of majuscules E, F, T, and some left head-serifs and foot-serifs, and one suspects that these similarities are the reason why some erroneously credit the reed with originating the serif. But, confronted with the other majuscules, serif- resemblance ends. Figure 135 shows the dis-

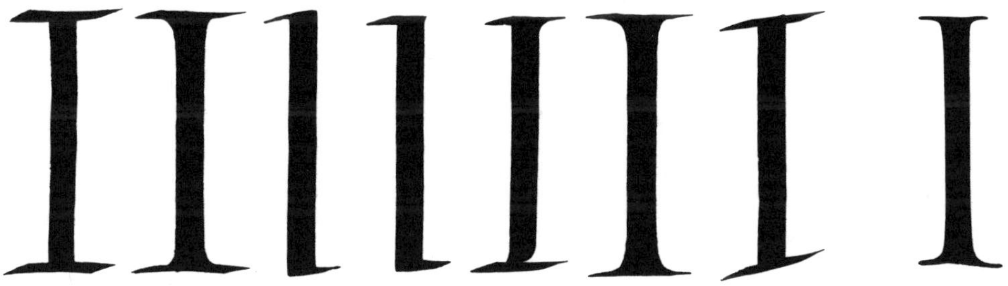

![Some reed-written and one chisel-cut majuscule letter I]

Fig. 135. Some reed-written and one chisel-cut, majuscule letter I.

•

similarities between the reed-written majuscule I's on the left and the chisel-cut Trajan I on the right.

Shaded reed writing, Rome's great invention, plainly was not the origin of the glyptic serif. But we should understand all about reed handling in order to grasp more clearly what followed to produce the glyptic serif.

133

20

Calligraphy in Rome

ach age has a variety of skilled and unskilled writing. No two people write alike. This was true in the Republic and is true today. The chief difference between our age and ancient Rome is that we have many more alphabetic models to study, copy and adopt where Rome had but one. The ordinary, everyday casual writing of all writers is informal. The usual distinction between the calligrapher and others is that the calligrapher has formal and semi-formal writing skills which he adopts for various purposes, whereas the cacographer and ordinary scribbler have not.

Yet despite the different external appearance of various kinds of writing practiced by the calligrapher, all his scripts usually have the same model as a mental pattern or prototype. What is the reason for several scripts, and, why not use the best script for all purposes?

According to our definitions of informal, semi-formal, and formal writing, we find that the use of one or another of these is chiefly due to the purpose envisioned. If the writing of the calligrapher is to be permanent, favoring the need of the reader who seeks well-made letters, the calligrapher takes care to make them clearly and legibly. If the writing is not intended to be permanent, favoring the need of the writer, he writes hastily scribbled letters. Formal letters favor the need of the *eye that reads,* whereas informal favor the *hand that makes* the letters. Speed of writing then is a chief cause for the shift from formality to informality in a calligrapher's writing. Figure 136 shows examples of the three kinds of writing by contemporary calligraphers.

Every new alphabetic script, though made with primitive skill and appearing crude to the prejudiced eye of the critical calligrapher, is

Written with the pen I use for all personal rapid

Handwriting & Calligraphy

a ITALICATILI

·

Rapid writing changes Roman letters

Rapid writing changes the Roman letters

b Rapid writing changes the Roman lette

·

yetvor bni Rhode lom yomit ellorp homg

entigr olim crati Rvoli ariedli

c dopite Pelo Benoatd fikel

Fig. 136. Informal, semi-formal, and formal writing
by present day calligraphers, Lloyd Reynolds (a),
James Hayes (b), and the author (c).

formal. The first archaic Latin script was formal. There are three known incunabula of Latin letters, written and lettered in the 7th-6th century B.C.: the "Praenestine Brooch," "Roman Forum Cippus" ('Lapis Niger,') and the "Duenos" pottery inscriptions. A brief description of these is in order. The Praenestine Brooch, a golden clasp dating from

Fig. 137. Praenestine Brooch, 7th century B.C. Full size. Rome, Luigi Pigorini Museum of Ethnography and Prehistory.

•

the 7th century B.C., is quite probably the oldest Latin inscription. It was found in Praeneste (modern Palestrina) an ancient center of Latin culture 25 miles southeast of Rome in 1871. The inscription MANIOS:

$$\text{IOIƧAMVИ:ᗡƎꓘAIHꟻ:ƎHꟻ:ᗡƎM:ꟄOIИAM}$$

Fig. 138. A stylized redrawing of the retrograde inscription on the Praenestine Brooch.

•

MED:FHE:FHIAKED:NVMASIOI: is retrograde and, in more modern Latin, reads as MANIOS ME FECIT NVMASIOI i.e., MANIOS MADE ME FOR NUMASIOS.

The Roman Forum Cippus was found in 1899 beneath the Roman Forum pavement of black marble (whence the name 'Lapis Niger') to the front of the Arch of Septimius Severus, at the supposed burial

136

Fig. 139. Two views of the Roman Forum Cippus, 7th-6th century B.C.

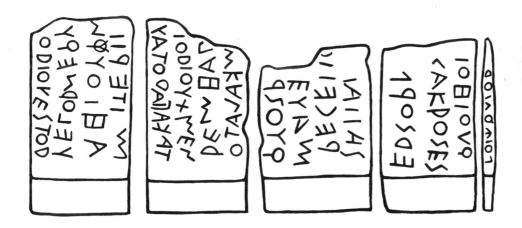

Fig. 140. A 'stretch-out' of the Roman Forum Cippus inscription. The inscription is retrograde, that is, with alternate (boustrophedon) left-to-right and right-to-left sentences.

site of Romulus. The Forum Inscription is cut on four sides and a champfered edge of a rectangular stone pillar, the top of which has been broken off or been chipped away, destroying part of the inscription, which runs vertically in alternate lines of right-to-left and left-to-right (boustrophedon) lettering.

The Duenos Vase (or *Vasculum Dressilianum* after Dr. Dressil who discovered it) was found in a Roman garden between the Viminal and Quirinal hills in 1880. It is made of three small clay vases combined into one body around which a retrograde inscription in archaic Latin, with no division between words, is inscribed. Since its discovery

Fig. 141. Two views of the Duenos Vase (Vasculum Dressilianum). Full size. Berlin, National Museum of Antiquities.

138

about fifty interpretations have been assigned to this inscription. It appears to have been destined as a love philtre or for some magical purpose.

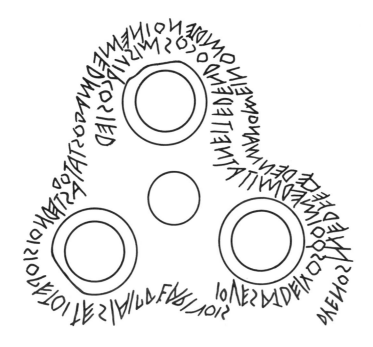

Fig. 142. A 'stretch-out' of the retrograde Duenos inscription.

•

These three inscriptions on brooch, pillar, and vase, have the marks we assign to formal writing: uprightness, clearcut distinction of parts

Fig. 143. Alphabet (lacking B) from the Roman Forum Cippus inscription, 7th-6th century B.C.

139

and letters, angularity, absence of ligatures and cursiveness, etc. This is to be expected. In the first age of the invention or adoption of an alphabet great care is taken to make copies correspond to the original model. In time readers and writers become familiar with the new invention and with familiarity resemblance to the original model decreases as sub-varieties and personal interpretations of the original increase. Familiarity and informal writing go hand in glove. This is more easily understood if we are aware of the part kinesthesis plays in writing.

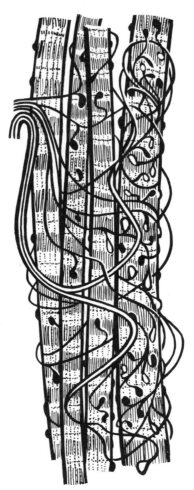

Fig. 144. Interoceptive nerve endings and muscle fibers.

In addition to the five exteroceptive senses of sight, hearing, touch, etc., we have the interoceptive and proprioceptive senses, which monitor the internal environment of the deeper regions of the body. These are activated by nerve processes within the organism itself. Among the proprioceptive are the pressure receptors of muscles, tendons, ligaments, joints, blood vessels and other internal organs. Proprioceptive nerve endings in many cases extend over the ends of muscle fibers or may encircle or spiral the muscle. In other cases the endings may be club-shaped or resemble circular plates. The nerve ends of tendons and ligaments show like variations of form; and in joints, definite bulbous endings, like tactile corpuscles, are found. The conscious reaction to these internal pressure receptors is called the muscle or *kinesthetic sense* for it makes us aware of our own motions.

Kinesthesis like the five exteroceptive senses is a true sense. One does not have to look at any part of his body to know whether muscles are contracted, or joints bent, or that the body is in a particular posture or action. The function of the kinesthetic sense is to keep the brain in-

Fig. 145. Ovals, curves, and slanted lines are more natural and easier to make than circles, horizontal and vertical lines.

141

formed of events taking place in one's muscles, joints, ligaments, and tendons, to help direct them, and to relieve the brain, in some part, of constant, tiresome, attention to such activity — that is, to act as an "automatic pilot," by-passing the mind and thus allowing the mind to attend to more important phases of the action of which the muscular-skeletal-tendonous activity is a part.

For example, if with my eyes shut I trace with my finger a figure eight in the air, I am able to know that it is a figure eight that my finger has traced. And if I wish to sign my name in the dark I am able to do so, because constant practice in the muscular action of making my signature has established in my mind the memory of that kinesthetic pattern. It is evident that all manual skills depend on kinesthetic patterns, and in no art is this more important than in that of calligraphy. In writing, kinesthesis is specifically concerned with the visible and invisible path traced by the hand holding the writing tool, stroke sequences and directions, the visuo-muscular memory and patterns of letters, the "follow through" of strokes, and the muscle-sense anticipation of letter parts about to be written.

In calligraphy, as elsewhere, a kinesthetic pattern is characterized by its causes. Chief among these are the limits imposed by the writing hand (and in the case of large letters, of the arms and legs) . These limbs are basically assemblages of jointed bones and muscles. Obviously the hand can make certain strokes more easily than others —— for example a diagonal stroke from upper right to lower left more comfortably and easily than a vertical or horizontal, a curved than a straight one, and a tilted oval more easily than a true circle. This explains why our informal, cursive writing slants to the right. In our daily writing we concentrate on the meaning of what we write rather than on the writing shapes themselves, with the result that we leave the shaping of the letters and words to our kinesthetic sense, which, when left to itself, finds the slant to the right its most natural inclination.

Slanting to the right, then, is one of the first traits of informal writing. Another is fusion of strokes and ligaturing. Still others are a rounding of angular shapes, a preference for stylographic tools, and,

142

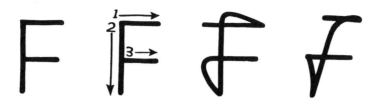

Fig. 146. The three essential strokes, sequence and direction of formal, majuscule F, and the two kinesthetic traces which (when hurriedly written) produce the one-stroke, minuscule f.

Fig. 147. A simplified condensation of the historical devolution of some majuscules into minuscules.

143

when square-edged hard tools are used, a tendency to maintain the same cant throughout a body of writing, to accent the thinnest edge stroke and to write at about 45 degrees cant.

In formal writing two essential parts of a letter are joined by the invisible kinesthetic trace. The calligrapher makes a conscious effort to keep these parts distinct by lifting his writing tool between these parts, thus keeping their connecting kinesthetic trace invisible. When the kinesthetic sense assumes control and writing shapes become familiar, it asserts its proneness to simplifying the kinesthetic trace so that what before in formal writing were three parts (two visible essential parts and their invisible connecting trace) now become one visible stroke. Figure 146 shows how letter F loses its formality (three essential strokes and two connecting kinesthetic traces,) and becomes informal (one stroke) [13] when the kinesthetic sense takes over.

Speaking generally kinesthesis is historically important, for it is at the root of the devolution of majuscules that produced minuscules — that is, the kinesthetic changeover from formality to informality in letter-making, and kinesthesis explains the formation of semi-formal (Italic) writing from formal writing (Fig. 136). Figure 147 shows how capitals, when written with correct stroke sequences, mutate informally into minuscules. The mutation of every lower-case letter from its formal majuscule occurred in this manner. Figure 148 shows letters D and R, taken from Pompeian wall inscriptions and wax tablets, in various

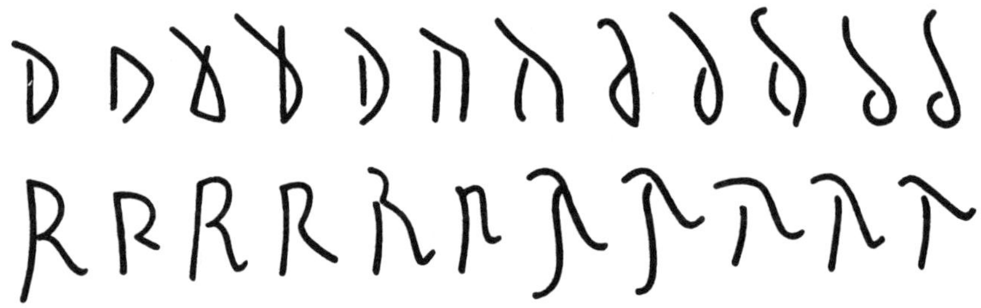

Fig. 148. Cursive letters D and R, written before the Vesuvian eruption in 79 A.D., taken from Pompeian wall inscriptions and wax tablets as shown in C.I.L. vol. XIV.

144

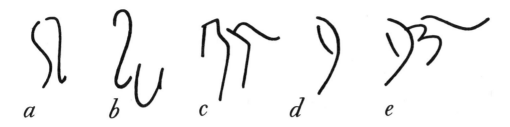

a   *b*   *c*   *d*   *e*

Fig. 149. Ligatures taken from informal writing on the Dacian Wax
Tablets, second century. The letters are: (a) GI; (b) BU; (c) PLAR;
(d) TI; (e) ERA.

•

stages of informality, and figures 150 and 151 show alphabets taken
from Pompeian graffiti and wax tablets with capital letters in various
stages in this mutation process. The Dacian Wax Tablet ligatures are
far removed from their majuscular prototypes (Fig. 149).

Fig. 150. An alphabet taken from Pompeian wax tablets.

•

Fig. 151. Alphabet taken from Pompeian wall-scribblings.

145

In the early days of Rome, shortly after shaded writing had been accepted as reading and writing fare by Romans, the three classes of writing existed. While we do not have definitive paleographic examples, thus far, of the three kinds of writing in the Republic, their existence is proven by the presence of ligaturing. For examples, ligatures appeared in Roman letters on coins about 200 B.C. and in inscriptions about 150 B.C. Furthermore the widespread distribution of various minuscular scripts in the first century suggests a long antecedent period of informal writing and great familiarity with alphabetic shapes. Edward Maunde Thompson says "It is probable that the wall-scribblings of Pompeii essentially represent the style of cursive writing which had been followed for some two or three centuries before their date; . . ."[14] (before the Vesuvian eruption of 79 A.D.) That is, Mr. Thompson believes it quite probable that cursive, informal writing was common in the third century B.C. and hence, at that time, a widespread familiarity with the three kinds of writing, informal, semi-formal, and formal.

The presence of several writing hands was not unique in Rome. David Diringer, writing in McGraw Hill's *Encyclopedia of World Art*, III, 13, reports that "As far back as the oldest preserved documents (4th cent. B.C.), we see side by side two classes of Greek cursive writing—the literary bookhand and the current or running hand, used for nonliterary writing (letters, accounts, receipts, etc.)." Since Roman literature was based on Greek models there is good reason for believing that Roman scribes also followed Greek calligraphic practice. Moreover Clement of Alexandria says 'that in the education of the Egyptians three styles of writing are taught: demotic, hieratic (sacerdotal), and hieroglyphic,' (Clem. Alex. Strom. v. vol. ii, p. 657.) —the hieroglyphic being formal, and demotic, the informal cursive script.

In writing, easily handled, simple tools like the stilus precede the reed, a more difficult tool, and both stilus and reed precede the brush, the most sophisticated and difficult of all writing tools. The stilus is mostly the informal writer's tool while the reed and brush are the tools of the calligrapher and professional scribe who express themselves usually in semi-formal and formal scripts.

146

We are not certain when the Roman scribe abandoned stilus tools and took up the square-edged reed to write shaded letters, in which horizontal letter parts were about one-half as thick as vertical ones. It would appear that it was adopted by professional or semi-professional scribes who had more than a casual, amateur interest in the well-making of letters. One reason immediately suggests itself, namely that the crisp, shaded-letter design quality, naturally produced by the reed, would have a greater appeal to professional scribes than would the monotonous, equal-width strokes of stilus writing. Indications are that the change from stilus to reed took place sometime in the second century B.C. In the changeover the basic skeletons of the script then in vogue were not radically changed. Following the lead of Professor Battelli of the Vatican Institute of Paleography and Diplomatics we call this primitive writing librarial, that is, the first shaded writing made by the Roman *librarii*. While we do not have samples of such writing its existence is clearly indicated by its sophisticated offspring, monumental letters, Rustic, and Square Capitals, which have this shaded reed writing in common.

Figure 152 is an example of third century stilus-written letters freely copied from the Tomb of the Scipios in the Vatican Lapidary Galleries. Figure 153 shows these same letters traced over with the reed to suggest the shapes the first Roman shaded letters assumed.

CORNELIOLFSCIPIO
IDILES COSOL CESOR

Fig. 152. Stilus letters copied from the funerary inscription of Consul L. Cornelius Scipio, 259 B.C. Vatican Lapidary Galleries.

•

CORNELIOLFSCIPIO
IDILES COSOL CESOR

Fig. 153. Third century stilus letters from the Tomb of the Scipios re-written with the square-edged reed to suggest the probable shapes of the first shaded Roman writing.

•

How long did this primitive reed letter, lacking embellishments, serifs, terminal flourishes, endure? We do not know. However, one can, by making a comparison with the time it takes to acquire an elementary, untutored reed writing technique today, conjecture that the primitive letter lasted but a short time, say, not more than a year or two, or until the scribe by practice with his new tools became proficient enough to attempt inventive expressions beyond the shaping of letters. Nor ought we to lose sight of the fact that the reed as a writing tool was known and used in the eastern Mediterranean and therefore not entirely a mystery to the Roman scribe.

Among Roman scribes, there were two groups who made letters — amateur scribes and professional calligraphers — the one making only

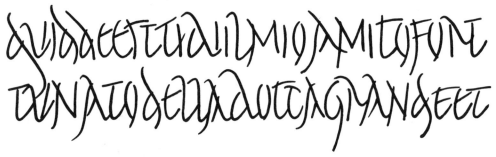

Fig. 154. Everyday, informal, Roman cursive writing made of random letters. First century.

148

informal letters, the other, in addition, writing formal and semi-formal letters. Amateur scribes writing informally would include students, teachers, authors, correspondents, and tradespeople. Their tools were pen and stilus and their writing materials were ink, clay, wax, slate, etc. Their informal writing would be casual, not intended for permanence, rapidly written, jerky, often with merged strokes, slurred letter-parts, and cursive joinings, curvilinear, slanted, compressed, with letter parts rising above and falling below head and base lines, and generally of the same stroke-thickness throughout. Figure 154 shows a haphazard grouping of first century Roman, cursive letters.

Professional scribes, whose chief occupation was making letters, were much fewer in number than the amateurs. In this group were sign writers, letterers, copyists, and *librarii,* the "printers," or publishers who wrote, collated, and bound into rolls *(volumina)* the work of such authors as Pliny, Juvenal, Plutarch, and others.

RVDIVASCLFAINEOSB

QVIODPATIVREOIVCE

SIQIRVTSPQVIDIGIAPBRVTQ

Fig. 155. Professional Square Capitals and Rustic writing.

•

Naturally Latin authors were anxious to have their works neatly and legibly published. Some authors had their own staff of calligraphers *(librarii)* and bookbinders *(glutinatores,* Cicero, *Ad Att.* iv, 4) who pasted the papyrus sheets into rolls. These librarial scribes were the calligraphic standardizers who wrote both formal and semi-formal lit-

149

erary bookhands and who undoubtedly, in their everyday, non-craft writing, made use of an informal writing as did Niccolõ de Niccoli, the Renaissance calligrapher who had several writing hands which he used for different purposes (Cf. fig. 136). The writing materials used by these Roman book publishing firms and their *librarii,* writing formal and semi-formal bookhands, were ink on papyrus and, in smaller quantities, parchment and vellum[15]. The writing tools were reeds and quill pens.

Now the first type-designers in the 15th century did not create their typefaces *ex nihilo,* as Dr. B. L. Ullman demonstrates in his definitive book, *The Origin and Development of Humanistic Script.* They appropriated as their model the better, formal, bookhands of the first half of their century — all traceable to Poggio Bracciolini, the inventor of the humanistic script. The sign writers and monument letterers in Rome did no less — they took over the better literary bookhand of their time. There was no reason for not using the script *familiar to all readers.* Professor Battelli confirms this, saying that "La scrittura rappresenta lo svolgimento calligrafico della capitale arcaica, parallelo a quello della capitale epigrafica." (*Lezioni di Paleografia,* Citta' del Vaticano, 1936, p. 46.) — that is, 'the librarial script and epigraphic capitals are a parallel development from archaic capitals.'

150

21

A theory of development and lineage for the Roman alphabet

fter the Imperial age there is no difficulty in tracing letter development and branchings. There is ample paleographic evidence to draw on. Our difficulty is trying to chart a reasonable branching back to alphabetic roots before the Imperium. In the light of the matter being discussed: the primacy of writing, lettering as an offshoot of the formal writing in all but the first age, inscription making as a sign writing expression of professional scribes *(librarii)*, the invention of shaded writing, and the Roman cant adoption, I suggest that alphabetic lineage may be traced in the manner shown in figure 161. Here a brief note on the parentage and infancy of Latin letters, before shaded writing became the national script of Rome; is appropriate.

Fig. 156. Marsilian abecedarium of Albegna, late eight or early seventh century B.C.Florence,Museum of Archeology.Full size.

The Etruscan alphabet, Graeco-Phoenician in origin, is the parent of the Latin alphabet. The most ancient abecedarium, dating from the end of the 8th or the beginning of the 7th century B.C., is the *Tavoletta Marsigliana d'Albegna* found in 1915 in a tomb near an Etruscan maritime center on the west coast of central Italy. It is made of ivory (2″ x 3.4″) with its center slightly depressed to receive wax and may be the prototype of later waxed tablets. Quite possibly it was a teaching device to aid the beginner in writing and spelling. On its upper border, inscribed from right to left, is a Greek alphabet of archaic form derived from the North Semitic alphabet from which it retains four sibilants *zayn* (soft *s*), *samek* (aspirate *s*), *tsade* (emphatic *s*), and *shin* (*sh*). Another abecedarium is the Formello Vase (also called *Amphora Chigi di Formello* after its finder Prince Chigi), which dates from the 7th cen-

Fig. 157. Formello amphora, 7th century B.C. (1/3).
Rome, National Museum of Villa Giulia.

•

tury B.C. It was found in 1882 at Formello near Veii and contains an Etruscan inscription and two complete alphabets of archaic Greek form.

152

arranged precisely in the accepted Semitic order, one alphabet near the lip and the other at the base of the black vase. Each alphabet also contains the Phoenician letters *samek* and *tsade*. The alphabet on the lip of the vase shows F before E but the alphabet at the base has E and F in their correct order.

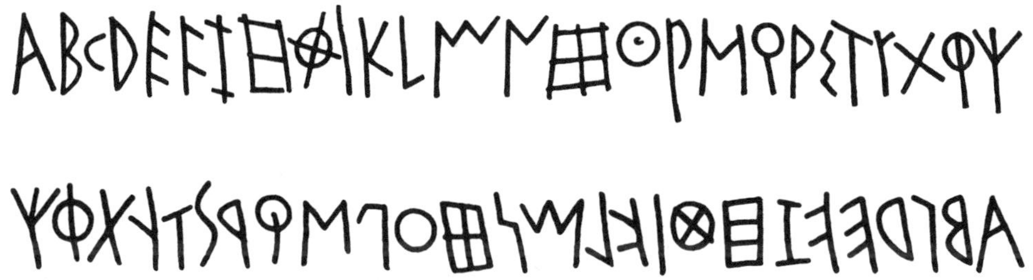

Fig. 158. Graeco-Phoenician, Etruscan alphabets from the Formello Vase (1) and the Marsilian Tablet (2).

•

These Graeco-Phoenician letters are the antecedents of the Archaic Latin Capitals which first appeared about the seventh century B.C. Archaic Latin capitals, like Etruscan capitals, were stilographic as on the *Praenestine Fibula,* the *Roman Forum Cippus* or marker ('Lapis Niger'), and the *Duenos Vase.* Such an alphabet, lacking B, is shown in

Fig. 159. Archaic Latin Alphabet from the Roman Forum Pillar.

•

figure 159. Professor Battelli says that 'two kinds of writing are directly derived from the archaic Latin capitals, the origin and mother of all subsequent letter forms, 1) cursive capitals, the everyday, informal writing, and 2) librarial capitals expressed in the more common *rustic*

153

bookhand and the calligraphically accurate *elegant* (Square Capitals) bookhand.'

•

> Dalla *scrittura capitale arcaica,* che é la forma piu antica della scrittura Latina e la scrittura madre di tutte forme che si sono avute poi, derivano direttamente due generi: *la capitale libraria* nei due tipe di *rustica,* d'uso piu commune, ed *elegante,* dalle forme piu accurate e calligrafiche: *la capitale corsiva,* usate come scrittura d'affari nelle lettere, nei documenti ecc. (Op. cit., p. 35.)

•

For several centuries after their adoption from the Etruscan (about the seventh century B.C.) practically nothing is known of the history of Latin letters. At the start of the third century considerable writing activity takes place, and the writing, though monolined, begins to show forth the basic skeletons of the later, thick-and-thin, monumental alphabet. Shaded reed writing is the characteristic Roman invention and the instrumental cause of the monumental alphabet of Rome. The change from stilographic to shaded writing occured, I am convinced, at the beginning of the second century B.C. This reed writing is conterminous with librarial (*libraria*), its book-publishing and notarial usage, from which developed all later, formal and informal scripts whether made with reed, quill pen, stilus, or brush, and of course, all inscriptional shapes. The presence in the third century B.C., of rudimentary serifs in inscriptions from Praeneste hints at the use of a square-edged brush or frayed reed which produced these terminals. In turn these Praenestine serifs suggest that shaded writing may have had its beginnings even earlier, in the second half of the third century B.C.[16]

The main stem of writing, and that most used, was informal cursive, the casual, commercial-epistolary script (*scriptura communis* or *epistolaris*) made with stilus tools on wax, clay, bark, etc. Formal writing, flanking informal in figure 161, had two main expressions, one, on the left, was the librarial calligraphy using *hard tools,* pen, and reed on papyrus, skins, and wax[17], the other, on the right, using chiefly *soft*

154

tools (frayed reeds and brushes) and making mostly larger letters for public display.[18].

Hard tool usage, the chief occupation of professional letter makers, was devoted primarily to small shaded writing for use in book-making, literary, secretarial and bronze tablet production. A small segment of these professional scribes, using the brush (soft tool) in place of the reed, without doubt became the sign writers who developed *scriptura actuaria,* the large display letters similar to those written on Pompeian and Roman walls, and *scriptura monumentalis,* the classic, imperial, written-then-chiselled, inscription letters.

Contrary to the usual idea of alphabet origin it is to be noted in this scheme that lapidary capitals do not occupy a position of origins, but instead lapidary capitals are placed at the side from which no writing hands issue. Not the least reason for showing lapidary work as a branch and not a main stem in figure 161 is quantitative. By far the greatest amount of writing was informal, everyday, cursive script, followed in lesser amount by formal and semi-formal librarial bookhands, with inscription work affording the fewest examples.

In the West there were two eras, each with a special reason, needing large display letters. These reasons are: 1) commemorative magnificence in architecture and 2) modern merchandising. Rome, with its large dedicatory, donative, honorary, promulgatory, and sepulchral needs, is clearly indicated as the one and contemporary display advertising as the other. This will explain why in the scheme of figure 161[19], lapidary letters are shown as terminal with no immediate progeny, for large, direct, brush writing vanished with the decline of Rome and did not rise again as a vital craft until the 20th century, when it is reborn as a merchandising art in our country.

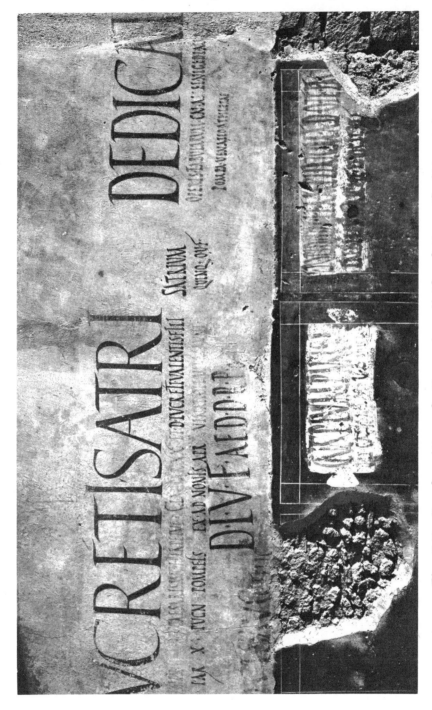

Fig. 160. Brush-written electioneering display letters (Scriptura Actuaria) from the house of Aulus Trebius Valens in Pompeii. First century. The large letters are almost two feet tall. A good part of this wall and its inscriptions were destroyed during a 1943 bombing. Photograph by courtesy of the Superintendent of Antiquities, Naples region.

156

Fig. 161. A theory for the development of
alphabetic expressions in early Rome and after.

22

Brush writing in Rome

uring the first and second centuries of our era, when the better Roman inscriptions were being made, Rome supported a thriving building industry that employed thousands of workers in the stone and marble trades —*Lapidarii, marmorarii, quadratarii.* Naturally there existed as well a vital inscription-making craft which occupied much the same position in that era that the sign writer and letterer occupy in our day. We might divide this group into three parts: sign writers, who brush-wrote the inscriptions; the sign letterers, who chiselled them; and the sign painters, who painted over the V-cut inscriptions. Of course in antiquity expertise in these three segments of the inscription process was not necessarily divided among several workmen—so common in our age of specialization. Indications are that ancient sign makers not only wrote but cut and painted their inscriptions.

We know little about these Imperial sign makers. We know of the existence of *scriptura actuaria* for the brush writing of wall signs (Fig. 160), public proclamations, electioneering placards, 'for sale' signs, gladiatorial games programs, contract announcements, ferial declarations, advertisements, 'lost and found' notices, cloth curtain signs, and even "newspapers"[20] recording births, deaths, buildings erected, festivals, fires, doings of the imperial family, amatory gossip and prodigies, from which we may deduce the presence of a sign craft making these. Painting 'black letters on a white ground' is mentioned in *Lex Acilia Repetundarum,* of the year 122 B.C. (*Corpus Inscriptionum Latinarum,* i² 2, 583, 14, *in tabula, in albo, atramento scriptos*), and large numbers of wall signs, painted in red and black, have been preserved in Rome and Pompeii. Martial tells Lupercus, in Epigram 117, Bk. 1., that his (Martial's) books can be bought, opposite Caesar's Forum, at the bookshop, whose 'doorposts from top to bottom bear advertisements,' "... *scriptura postibus hinc et inde totis...*"

It is not illogical to suppose that sign writers and inscription makers were a branch of *librarii* or *ex-librarii* who specialized in large brush writing: still using their formal and semi-formal, librarial bookhands in new contexts and materials and, in the process, making technical adjustments.

Once the Roman calligrapher moved over into the sign-making trade the larger letters called for different tools. One can write with a reed on polished stone, but it is not suited to writing on boards, stuccoed walls, or rough stone, since there is no give to such surfaces and very little to the reed. A tool with more adaptability is needed. The square-edged brush, actually a large, flexible extension of the reed, quite naturally suggested itself. It was just the thing for large letters, could carry a larger load of paint, write longer without recharging and, unlike the reed, which requires paper-smooth surfaces for writing, could write on rough surfaces.

In point of fact the problem of achieving monumental and actuarial letter shapes was mainly technical, that is, a shift from small reed writing to large brush writing. In truth, skill, both mental and neuro-muscular, was already present having been acquired in the hard-tool apprenticeship. It is inconceivable that the monumental chisel-cut letter arose, fully fashioned like Aphrodite out of misty foam. The monumental alphabet shows unmistakedly its lineal descent from shaded writing. Its development from reed writing of 25-30 degrees cant into brush writing did not take much time, perhaps no more than a year or two. This is further supported by the lack of a transitional letter between the two, from the very nature of brush-written letters echoing the general shapes of letters fixed by the reed, and from the retention of the 2 : 1 proportion of vertical stems to horizontal arms which carried over into monumental brush writing.

Historically several varieties of brush letters co-existed and not infrequently were found on the same inscription, for example, figure

159

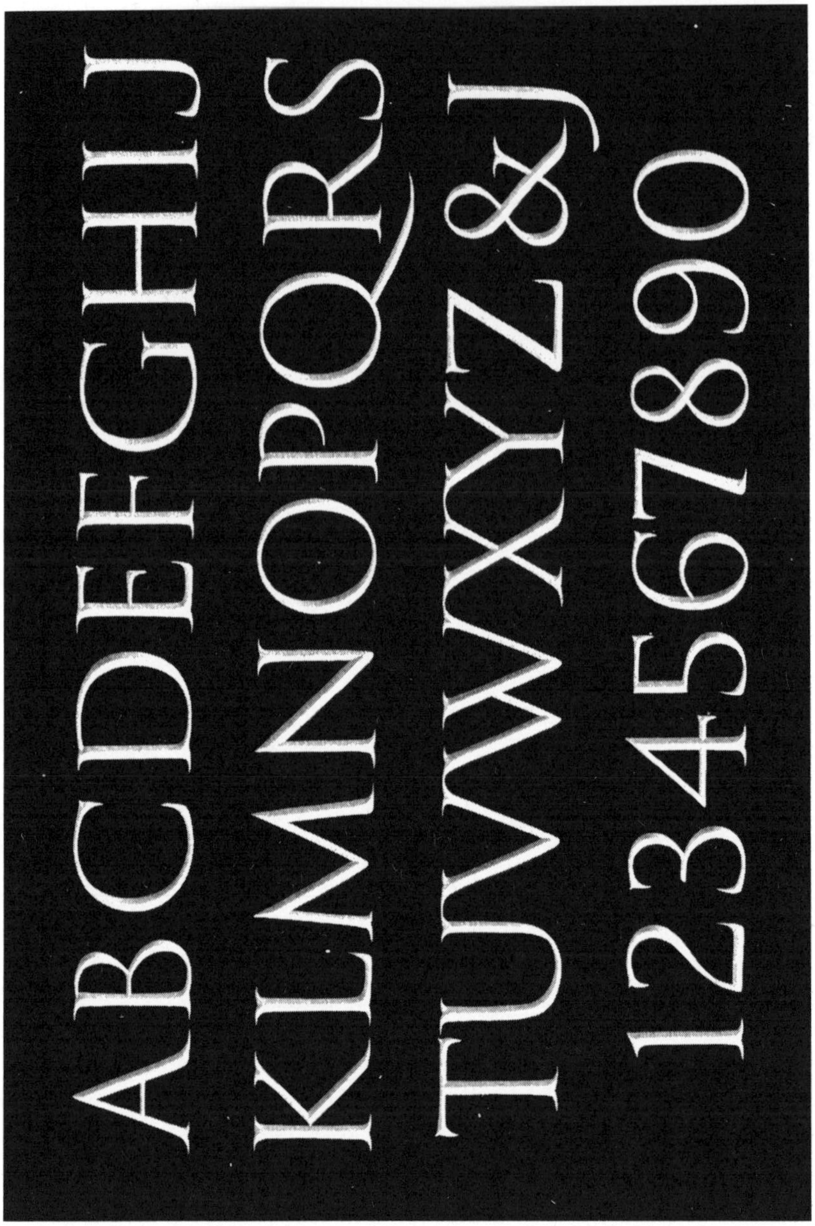

Fig. 162. Scriptura Monumentalis.

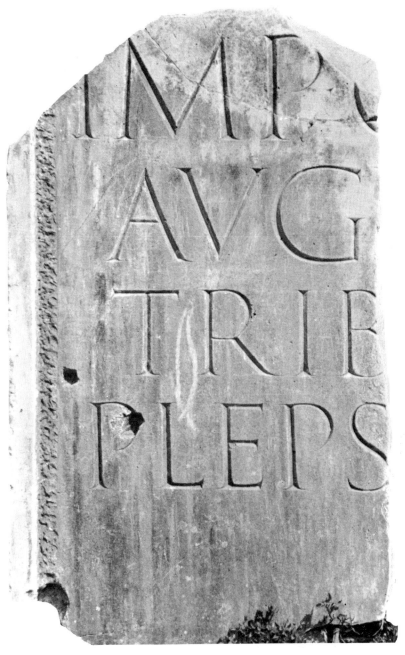

Fig. 163. Augustan inscription in the Roman Forum. 1 B.C.

112, the Trajanic inscription ((105 A.D.) now in the National Museum of Rome. The differences among them were of degree not kind and mixed scripts in the same inscription were not uncommon. The two most prominent were *scriptura actuaria,* the semi-formal, quickly written, sign writing for temporary display purposes and *scriptura monumentalis* (our chief interest), the formal, elegant, carefully made, permanent sign writing generally incised in stone. In the last statement "generally" is inserted for the reason that although we do not as yet have clearly defined examples of *painted scriptura monumentalis,* there is no doubt whatever that some monumental letters were painted only and not incised. This view of painting only and not incising is substantiated if one interprets Petronius' statement in *Satyricon* 28 (". . . in pariete . . . quadrata littera scriptum . . .") to mean 'monumental letters painted on the wall.' The large letters in figure 160, especially letters A, D, I, R, and S, along with their serifs, approach very closely to the best, chisel-cut monumental letters. These letters are more than twice the height of the tallest (letters M and P in the first line—11″ tall), chiselled, Augustan letters in the Roman Forum. (Fig. 163).

Here it is pertinent to state the general traits of this *scriptura monumentalis.* One trait is *economy of parts,* in which only necessary letter parts are retained. Another trait is that these parts, whether vertical, horizontal, or curved, are crisply stated, and *clearly differentiated* from each other. Still another trait is *economy of function,* in which every part makes its contribution in the exact amount and place to the overall unity of the letter. Still other traits are uprightness, restraint, invisible traces, absence of ligatures, less spontaneity and greater care in making, the 2 : 1 proportion of thick and thin parts, more reliance on a standardized shape and the exclusion of all romantic elements, swashes ,decorative factors, and personal calligraphic whims.

23

The brush & its handling

ne can imagine Roman sign makers in their first attempts at brush writing trying to make their square brushes behave like reeds. Very quickly, however, they discovered that brush writing was quite different from reed writing; and that the brush gave new dimension to calligraphic expression. As with any craft, the new technical achievements with the brush soon became the possession of all the skilled members of the Roman sign trade.

Now the reed writer making small letters is confined chiefly to the movements of his fingers, which in turn restrict him practically to one, constant cant angle. An increase in reed and letter-size will engage the larger joint behind the fingers, the wrist, and also allows for a slight modification away from a fixed cant.

The brush writer making still larger letters will engage the larger joints of his writing arm — the elbow, and shoulder joints. The use of these larger joints permits the writer a still wider scope in cant. It is quite possible in writing letters, say, six feet tall, to use not only the joints of the writing arm, but the vertebral, hip, knee, and ankle joints, and in so doing to make changes from and into any cant angle.

Other factors also enter into brush writing which alter its character. Chief of these is the kind of hair it is made of, its length, quantity and arrangement. Thus short hog bristles, because of their stiffness, allow little movement among the bristles. A square brush made of hog hair, having little pliability, is not very different from a large reed.

But a square brush made of red sable (kolinsky hair, *mustela siberica*) is considerably more pliable than the hog bristle and therefore capable of more internal movement. Of course the longer the hair the more inner action and motion. This explains why long, pointed, brushes are called *outlining* or *scroll* brushes, for when loaded with paint their pliability makes possible graceful curves, scrolls, long drawn-out ascenders and descenders as well as spikey serifs.

Fig. 164. Strokes made directly in one movement of the brush, with many changes of cant, and with no retouching or retracing of strokes.

164

Fig. 165. Changes of cant made in one stroke.

165

A sign writer using a half-inch–wide square, chisel-edged brush, and writing letters four inches tall, can change his cant at will, not only in making individual letters, but for the various parts of a single letter. In fact it is not uncommon for a brush writer to change his cant from zero to ninety degrees and back again or the reverse, all in one rapid movement of the brush as is demonstrated in figure 164. Figure 165 shows additional but more complicated possibilities in cant changes and brush twirling. These up-down, down-up, forward–backward, cant-gyrating strokes are wholly natural to the chisel-edged brush and pleasing to the brush writer to make,and cannot be made by the square pen, reed, 2-pencil marker, or any hard, edged tool. These strokes have been written in one movement or stroke of the brush without lifting the brush from the paper and, of course with no retracing or retouching.

slow writing   *fast writing*

Fig. 166. Fast writing produces a narrower brush stroke.

•

Unlike the reed, the brush is held almost upright, perpendicular to the writing surface, as is customary in Chinese calligraphy. This greatly aids the frequent changes in cant and allows the workman to write in all directions. In normal use the hair tips of the brush trail or

166

flow along behind the ferrule and handle of the brush. When the brush is held at a slant, like a pen, pencil or reed, the direction of strokes is limited. In such a position the brush cannot be worked against the hair tips for it will spurt, thus splattering the paint. The brush writer generally holds the chisel-shaped brush lightly, and to effect changes in cant, twirls it between thumb and forefinger.

The fact is not generally understood that various parts of letters are made in varying speeds and rhythms, and that even in one stroke there are many tempo-changes[21]. Some letter parts are made rapidly, others more slowly. In general, horizontal bars are made more quickly than vertical stems and curves more slowly than straight parts although the tail of Q is the fastest and perhaps easiest of all strokes to make. Among letters, S is the slowest to make, and, for that reason, the first to become misshapen in rapid writing.

One quickly learns that strokes in reed writing start slowly, speed up in their mid-sections and end slowly, and that the terminal flick at the right bottom of the stems (the follow-through, so to say) is the fastest part of the stroke.

First strokes are easier and quicker to make than subsequent strokes and, excepting tails, usually the most exacting stroke is the last, since it must relate with letter parts previously made. As an example, the left half of majuscule O, limited only by the guide lines, is fashioned more rapidly than the right half. The right half is disciplined by the guide lines, the two ends of the left curve and by its own shape. By far the slowest part of O to make is the ending of the right curve which must meet and relate exactly with the bottom end of the left curve.

There are resemblances and differences between the handling of the reed and brush. The chief difference in handling is that the reed has a fixed width which makes its widest strokes of an unvarying width; whereas the brush, in making full strokes, widens and narrows with the speed of the stroke and with its pressure on the writing surface. In reed writing, moreover variations in movement are mostly linear in a plane parallel to the writing surface whereas in brush writing a new, up-and-down dimension akin to Chinese brush handling, is present. When the

167

brush moves quickly the hair tips bend and trail directly behind the bent hairs aiding in the fast depositing of paint. But when it moves slowly the tips do not bend so much allowing the brush hair to spread laterally and permitting a more leisurely deposit of pigment. Thus a quickly written stroke will be slightly narrower than a slowly written one.

Fig. 167. Oblique stroke of S showing bottom swelling.

•

For example there is a slight swelling in the oblique stroke of S as the brush slows down just before making its turn to the left to meet the bottom arm of S (Fig. 167). In the tail of R there is a similar subtle swelling at the bottom just before the brush makes its turn to the right to begin its finishing stroke, and, in the like spot and for the same reason, a swelling is often found in the thick obliques of A, M, N, X, and V.

It is true that one could omit the slow-down before ending the

168

stroke, and amateur brush writers often do so. The result however is a thick, uneven, ragged stroke made by the "toe" rather than tip of brush. Since crisp brush strokes end along the thin edge, the brush must slow down to allow the hair tips to return to their normal position. Other

Fig. 168. Non-professional stroke ending.

parts of letters show the same brush dynamics, for example, the horizontals in C, E, G, L, R, S, T, and the numeral mark. The fillet between horizontal arms and vertical, terminal serifs is the natural *recovery* path traced by the brush tips moving into the terminal position. This also constitutes an additional proof of the priority of writing over lettering which has been discussed on page 110 f. Not only this swelling, but also the development of fillets and serifs depends on the single *premier coup* stroke. Taken together these three elements indicate that Imperial letters were written, and with a flexible, chisel-edged brush, and that stencils and other non-writing tools were not used.

24

Unreasoned bias against the brush

Misconceptions and faulty theories about writing and lettering interact and feed on each other so that it is difficult to disentangle them to discover which is cause, which effect. Yet one can reasonably say that the chief obstacles to recognizing the brush-origins of inscription letters and their serifs are: 1) a snobbish attitude towards sign writers and their work; 2) the ignoring by calligraphers, skilled in hard-tool writing (reed, pen, quill), of the soft, flat brush as a writing tool; 3) authors dismissing the brush by considering it to be a minor expression of the reed and square pen, thus 4) by-passing the unique ability of the writing brush to *change cant at will* during use.

For example, here are some statements from lettering texts written by the leading calligraphers of our time:

•

The flat brush is used in the same way as the pens and the two-pencils which have been described. It is not important here to go further into the description and use of brushes. Their popularity comes more from the needs of the show-card writer than the refined requirements of the letter designer. Acceptable brush lettering really depends more on dexterity than on a knowledge of form.

Warren Chappell, *The Anatomy of Lettering*, p. 4.

•

It is hard for the sign-writer to admit that his brush had nothing whatever . . . to do with the technical development of the Roman alphabet . . .

Graily Hewitt, *Lettering*, p. 23.

Brush writing as such has no real place in our study as it is primarily in the province of the show card writer and is not concerned with good, historically founded forms . . . practice with a chisel-shaped brush is splendid training for the hand, but the broad pen or double pencil is by far the better instrument for study.

Oscar Ogg, *An Alphabet Source Book*, p. 37.

It is instructive to discover the esteem in which letter designers and their tools, the reed and pen, are held, the lack of esteem shown to sign and show card writers, and the total dismissal of the brush as having had 'nothing whatever' to do with the formation and development of the Roman alphabet.

25

The action of the brush

ractice with the chisel-shaped brush calls for certain types of manipulation, and this practice establishes in the writer's mind corresponding kinesthetic patterns. These muscle patterns in turn become pyschologically attached to the visual pattern which the paint-charged brush leaves behind it on the prepared surface. The brush, then, acts as a physical link between two kinds of image—the visual and kinesthetic. The stroke of the calligrapher is as direct and unstudied as the stroke of a tennis champion with his racquet. In both cases the action is rapid and sure and is the result of endless disciplined practice. To suppose, for example, that the Trajan Inscription was laid out by means of stencils, or any such mechanical device, is tantamount to supposing that the tennis cup winner calculates the elements of his serve with a computer and slide rule. What are some of the visuo-kinesthetic elements out of which the good calligrapher composes his letters?

Fig. 169. Brush stroke without edge-in.

Like the reed, the square brush begins each wide stroke by contacting the surface with its thin edge at right angles with the stroke. To begin, for example, a vertical stem without this initial movement would result in an ugly, uneven stroke as shown in figure 169. The sign writer, even when making sans-serif letter stems, gives a very short, barely visible, horizontal wiggle to the beginning and ending of each visible stroke.

Fig. 170. Sign writer's "Egyptian" (sans-serif) letter.

•

The making of this little initial stroke is called "edging-in."[22] When the brush is lifted from the surface there is a corresponding process of "edg-

Fig. 171. Edging-in and edging-out.

173

ing-out," which leaves behind a little terminal stroke also. Of course, those strokes the start or ending of which are covered by other letter parts may dispense with these edging-strokes.

But every finish stroke, regardless of its direction or angle of cant, begins with the edge-in and ends with the edge-out flick of the brush. It is easiest to make this initial edging-in stroke about half the width of the brush in length. The terminal flick or edging-out stroke at the bottom of stems, obliques and arms will be longer.

174

26

The arm serif

owever, on examining inscription letters, the question might be asked: why is there such a broad stem serif? Could not a short serif have served as well, particularly since only a short edge-in stroke is needed? The clue is to be found in the edge-out (arm-serif) stroke of the thin horizontal arm—the one letter part that may be said to determine the 'style fix' or basic character of classic inscription letters.

When shaded book script is written small, the cant, once established, is generally held at that angle throughout the writing (Cf. pages 127 and 183). In small writing neither reader nor writer is unduly disturbed by the canted ends of stems and arms. But when letters are made large the angled cant of stems and arms becomes conspicuous and appears awkward (Fig. 172). Something must be done. The obvious corrective is to vary the cant and make endings perpendicular to shafts and arms as in figure 173. The reed writer does something akin to this when

Fig. 172. Large brush letters made with no change of cant to simulate reed-made letters.

175

he serifs or swirls arm and stem endings described on page 132 and shown in figures 133 and 134.

Fig. 173. Squaring off the canted ends of the large brush letters in figure 172.

•

The same problem faces the brush wielder writing large inscription letters on stone. He finds that canted endings will not do, are contrary to the classic ideal of simplicity, appear ungainly, and make *added work* for the letter cutter who must make two corners to the tops of letters E, P, R, etc. (Fig. 172).

It is true that the brush-writer could end arms with the natural edge-out stroke in the manner of semi-formal, Rustic letters. And in fact, as a writer acquires moderate skill, he finds that the edge-in and

Fig. 174. 'Rustic' letters, a natural tendency of brush writing when the writer becomes moderately skillful.

176

edge-out strokes tend, kinesthetically, to assert themselves and that his writing naturally assumes a 'Rustic' semi-formal character in which horizontal arms lose their rigid perpendicularity with stems and take on a double-curved, reversed-S, shape.

Rustic, like all semi-formal writings, is derived from a formal script. Whether Rustic was first a reed or brush letter is difficult to say. The reversed-S shape of arms, head and foot serifs is clearly a brush writing need. Naturally Rustic 'horizontals' can be made with the reed but they do not seem to fit the manipulatory feel of square-edged, hard tools as readily. The ease of writing Rustic letters with soft tools may have induced calligraphers to adopt Rustic for hard tool librarial writing. In either event one is on somewhat surer ground suggesting that Rustic is the bridge between hard tool librarial writing and soft tool monumental inscription writing for the obvious reason that monumental brush writing is strictly a professionally refined brush skill developed out of amateur, semi-formal brush handling. Of course professionals, as part of their repertoire, could write and cut Rustic and did so in many inscriptions. However the romantic, calligraphic character of Rustic is dissonant with the restrained formality demanded by classic, monumental letter making. The classic solution is to square off the endings as in figure 173. Ordinarily, though, such squaring off demands retracing and reworking of letters.

A corollary to the classic trait of economy of function is *economy of kinesthesis* in which the workman, after long familiarity with means and materials, reduces his movements to a minimum, avoids wasted motion and achieves his end in the most direct and efficient manner. In monumental letter making, the brush writer eventually learns that he too like the reed writer who adds the reed twirl (Figs. 133, 134) to his skills, can end horizontal arms more neatly, all in one stroke of the brush by acquiring the technically related but much more difficult skill of brush twirling combined with edging-out.

To do this the writer begins, for example, E's upper arm at the usual 25-30 degrees cant. As he nears the end of the arm, and using the right corner of the brush as a moving pivot point, he deftly and quickly twirls the left edge of the brush in a counter-clockwise movement from the normal cant into a downward, edging-out stroke of 90 degrees cant, all the while making certain that the right corner of the brush (the moving pivot point which also makes the upper outline of the arm)

Fig. 175. E's arm and serif written in one stroke of the brush.

continues its short straight path to the end of the arm. Figure 175 shows the upper arm of E made in such a stroke, and figure 176 shows the up-

Fig. 176. Arm serifs of C, E, F, G, L, and S, each written directly in one stroke with no retouching or retracing.

178

per arms of C, E, F, G, and S and the bottom arm of E, and L each made in like manner although some of these strokes begin at a cant differing from that of E's arm.

Earlier it was stated that normal (25-30 degrees) cant for Roman letters is such that it produces horizontal strokes about one-half as thin as vertical stems. This does not mean that every brush stroke must begin inexorably with this cant. Cant varies little when writing with the reed but when writing with the brush it varies considerably from zero to about 150 degrees. For example, the edge-in and edge-out stroke for vertical stems is near zero degrees producing, horizontal serifs. Some brush strokes, such as those for arms of C, G, and S (Fig. 176), edge-in at about 90 degrees, move into the normal cant for the horizontal segment of the arm, and edge-out in the vertical, down-pointing serif. And one stroke, the bottom arm of E and L, begins at about 150 degrees cant so that it may edge-out in a vertical, upward–pointing serif. But, despite the brush-writer's use of edging-in and -out strokes, the overall 2 : 1, thick-to-thin, proportion-relationship, (resulting from the characteristic Roman cant of 25-30 degrees) persists.

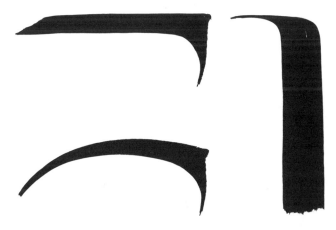

Fig. 177. Arm-serif determines serif-scaling.

•

A vertical stem with a short edge-in and edge-out stroke is understandable since the direction of the -in and -out strokes is perpendicular to the shaft of the thick vertical stem. But it is impossible to make a short edge-in stroke perpendicular to the thin horizontal arm of letter E. All edge-out and edge-in strokes must be made along the thin edge of the brush. The shortest possible serifs (edge-out strokes) on E's arms would be wider than E's thickest stroke, the stem, and at least twice as wide as the thin horizontal arms. Since the natural, edge-out stroke (serif) on E's arm cannot be shortened it becomes the *basic absolute,* determining serif-scaling throughout. And, in making this arm-serif, it is also impossible to avoid making the round fillet connecting the arm with serif.

Such "long" serif-endings are found in the horizontal arms of C, E, F, G, L, S, T and the numeral mark; in the thin oblique of A, M, X, and the tails of Q and R; in P's lobe-end and (present as a 'long' though hidden edge-out) in the lobe-ends and curves of B, C, D, G, O, Q, R, and S. Thus we have a total of 17 of 19 Trajan letters, plus the numeral sign, visibly (and all round letter parts kinesthetically) affected — enough to determine a calligraphic style trend.

But to mix normal, long serifs ending horizontal arms with short serifs of vertical stems plainly will not do. Hence the stem-serifs are broadened to preserve the relationship fixed by the arm-serifs.

The Imperial sign writer, without adverting to it, made fillets after the edge-in and before the edge-out strokes. The fillet, or modulatory curve between serif and stem or arm, is the natural product of the trailing hair tips of the brush as it moves from the edge-in stroke to the stem, and, the reverse. One could omit the fillet and make instead a sharp angle between the horizontal edge-in and vertical stem as in reed writing, but this would require a planned brush halt or two strokes — clearly contrary to fast, professional brush-writing, as any sign writer will affirm. But, in horizontal arms, one *cannot omit* the connecting fillet between arm and serif. Here the fillet is essential; and hence, like the arm-serif, a calligraphic standard for other letter parts.

Indeed one could emphasize the "basic absolute" nature of the brush-written, arm-fillet-serif stroke of letter E by stating that, once learned, this is the most satisfyingly natural stroke the brush makes,

180

and is apt therefore as the characteristic determinant of Roman brush-written *scriptura monumentalis*. Moreover, *this use of the brush is the key to the origin of the Roman serif.*

27

Reed & brush summarized

ur discussion over the past several chapters has revolved around the reed and brush, what they have, and do not have in common. Inasmuch as the brush has been likened to the reed and dismissed by calligraphic authorities as of no importance whatever in paleographic-epigraphic history, it is to the point to bring together here, side by side, the chief attributes of these two writing tools.

SUMMARY

REED	BRUSH
1. is held at a slant like pen or pencil	1. is held upright in the Chinese manner perpendicular to writing surface and
2. and makes strokes from top to bottom and left to right;	2. makes strokes in any direction;
3. is a hard writing tool;	3. is a soft writing tool;
4. apt for small writing;	4. apt for large writing;
5. with no 'give' on hard surfaces;	5. its internal pliability adjusts to rough stones, stucco, etc.;
6. carries a short load of ink;	6. carries a large load of pigment.
7. makes abrupt changes from thick to thin;	7. The change from thick to thin, is slow and gradual;
8. produces short tails	8. producing long, graceful tails
9. and flat curves.	9. and rounded curves.

10. Reed stroke is unchanging in width;

11. tends to be held at a constant cant;

12. usually produces sharp, internal angles at stroke junctures;

13. ungainly, outer oblique junctures;

14. mandorla-shaped counters;

15. and harsh, varying serifs.

10. Brush stroke varies in width with writing speed and pressure;

11. allows for frequent changes of cant;

12. makes soft, internal angles at stroke junctures;

13. round, uniform, outer junctures of obliques in A, M, N, and V;

14. and rounded counters.

15. Every visible brush stroke begins with the edge-in, ends with the edge-out stroke, and, in the process, produces consistent, regularly shaped, fillets and serifs.

28

Brush & inscription letters

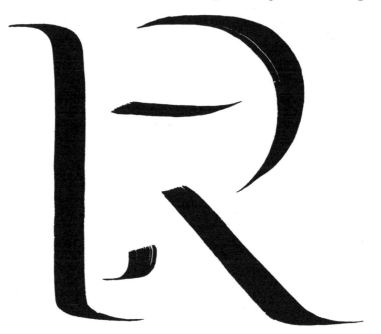

Reed writing contains no counterparts for the items native to the brush under no. 15 just listed. These are *unique to the brush*. Once these fundamentals of edging-in and edging-out, thumb-and-finger twirling to change cant, up-and-down pressure, and fillet production are understood, we can see the identity between brush-written and chiselled letters, that is, Rome's *littera monumentalis*.

The letter R, for instance, is the alphabet's most complex letter. It contains stem, lobe, arm, tail, cant changes, sharp internal angle, lobe

Fig. 178. The five parts of brush-written R.

Fig. 179. Four written R's.

and mid-arm juncture, two dents, mid-arm, head-, foot-, arm- (hidden in lobe and mid-arm), and tail-serifs. Directly R's stem, with its left head- and right foot-serif is written, it is not hard to see the need for a balancing left foot-serif.

Once we establish an identity between the brush-written and chisel-cut R, it is clear that similar identities can be fixed for the remaining, less complex letters of the Imperial alphabet.

●

THE DENT

In the literature of paleography, epigraphy, and calligraphy, I have been able to find no mention of the dent which appears between left and right head- and foot-serifs; between serifs and lobes of letters B, D, P, and R; between serifs and arms of E, R, and L. This dent ap-

Fig. 180. Dents in brush-written Imperial letters.

●

pears to be of minor value which may be the reason it receives neither recognition[23] nor explanation. On page 32, in another connection, I have already discussed this dent. It is a shape not consciously sought by the brush-writer. It is the juncture of two brush strokes. For example,

186

letter R has two such dents, one between head-serif and lobe, the other between left and right foot-serifs. The dent is plainly visible in the written R's (Figs. 178 and 179) and is a clinching proof for the brush-writing origin of serifs and letter parts.

•

THE LOBE-MID-ARM ANGLE

There is another element which, like the dent, has escaped notice, namely the rounded, internal angle where arms meet lobes in letters B, R, and (less noticeably) in D. Here again the brush is the sole reason

Fig. 181. The internal angles of B and R.

•

for these internal junctures. The upper lobe of B is written in the same sequence and direction as that of R. The bottom lobe of B begins at the juncture of arm and lobe and thus accounts for the internal angle of arm and lower lobe. The lobe of R starts from the stem at about 25 degrees cant, gradually changes cant to about 80 degrees in the thickest section at the upper right of the lobe and edges out to the bottom left at about 25 degrees. The mid-arm stroke edges out to the right and up to meet the lobe, thus shaping the sharp, inner, curve juncture so charac-

187

teristic of all well-written Imperial R's and B's. The inner juncture of letter D is not as pronounced in either B or R because the longer and wider lobe and arm makes a smoother modulation possible.

•

THE INTER-POINT

The simplest character in the Trajan Inscription is the inter-point or word separator. This also gives convincing proof for the brush-writing origin of inscription letters in general, and in particular for the serif.

Fig. 182. A Trajan inter-point.

•

Each Roman letter has its own specific proportions and orientation, that is, a Roman letter may not be written in mirror reverse, nor upside down, shortened, condensed, extended or varied in the relationship of its letter parts. But the inter-point has no fixed orientation nor does it

Fig. 183. Some brush-written inter-points.

•

Fig. 184. Inter-points from the age of Caesar, first century B.C., which appear to have been made in two strokes.

188

have an unalterable shape. Its only purpose was to separate words. It could have been any shape, and of these the simplest to chisel is the triangle. Yet of the many positions for a triangle only a special one was chosen, one that coincides with the cant common to brush-written Roman letters.

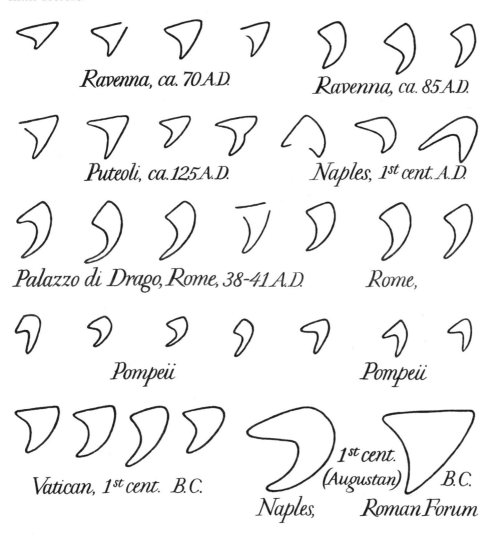

Ravenna, ca. 70 A.D.

Ravenna, ca. 85 A.D.

Puteoli, ca. 125 A.D.

Naples, 1st cent. A.D.

Palazzo di Drago, Rome, 38-41 A.D.

Rome,

Pompeii

Pompeii

Vatican, 1st cent. B.C.

Naples,

1st cent. (Augustan)

Roman Forum

B.C.

Fig. 185. Imperial inter-points from different places and times with various cant angles. Full size.

189

The base of the inter-point is the normal edge-in stroke of the brush. With the right corner of the brush acting as a moving pivot and, all the while twirling the brush in a counter-clockwise direction, the left side is formed and finally, with the edge-out flick to the left, the third or right side of the triangle is made (Fig. 183). I have seen a few inter-points which seem to have been made in two strokes, for example, the fourth point of those from Puteoli of around the year 125, shown in figure 185 and those in figure 184. Most points, however, were made in one stroke as the remaining examples in figure 185 show.

The general pattern in the calligrapher's mind is the triangle but the exigencies of his tool, the brush, and its natural workings, form the inter-point we now see in the Trajan Inscription. The Trajan writing master does not try, meticulously, to shape a geometrically equilateral triangle. Instead the inter-point as it now stands is a natural brush-written triangle made in *one stroke,* and hence, definitive corroboration of the primacy of writing over chiselling. Figure 185 shows some points taken from other, fine Imperial inscriptions which further confirm the continuous existence, over several centuries, of the Roman practice and belief that writing was the important ingredient and not lettering (chiselling) in the inscription making process. Note, in figure 185, that some inter-points are taken from Rustic (70-80 degrees cant), the rest from monumental inscriptions and that all point, at the bottom, to the left in the characteristic and natural, brush, edge-out direction.

•

The 'L' Stroke

Another argument for the brush is found in the slight obliquity of some letter parts away from the normal, vertical-horizontal alignment. This is noticeable in the 'L' stroke of letters B, D, E, and L. It is most pronounced in D, where the stem is not vertical as one might expect but has instead a minute backward slant.

The explanation is this: the long, terminal stroke of the stem is kinesthetically anticipated while making the vertical stem. This is not ordinarily evident in the vertical stem with its shorter edge-out stroke, but, when the edge-out lengthens into a letter part, as it does in letters

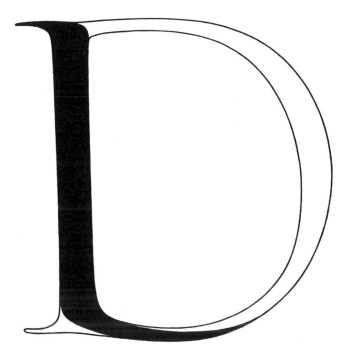

Fig. 186. The 'L' stroke of letter D.

•

B, D, E and L, the kinesthetic anticipation asserts itself unconsciously and this more so the longer the edge-out stroke. But the longest edge-out stroke is in letter D. Figure 187 shows the most obvious slant of the six D's in the Trajan Inscription — the fourth D in the fifth line.

The intuitive foreseeing of strokes or letter parts is not unique to D. It is present to a slight degree also in the thick oblique of M, N, and V, whose underside shows a delicate curvature as it joins the thin oblique of M, and V, and the right stem of N.

•

191

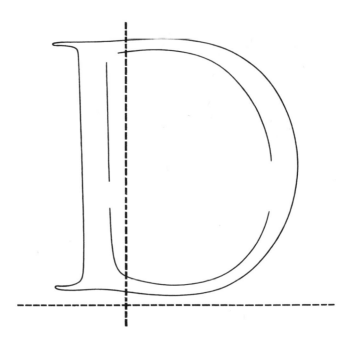

Fig. 187. The fourth D in the fifth line of the Trajan Inscription. The dotted lines show the vertical-horizontal alignment of the fifth line.

Fig. 188. The long edge-out stroke produces the rounded, bottom juncture in letters B, E, and L, as well as D (Fig. 186).

192

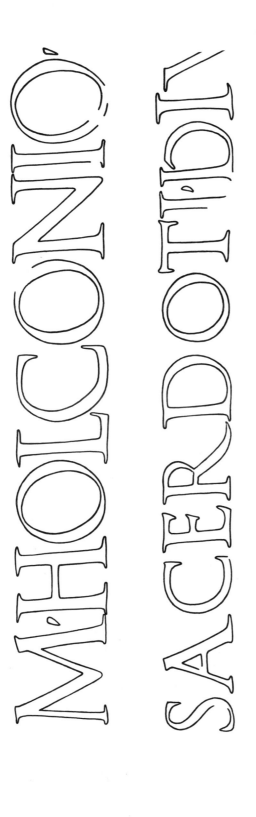

Fig. 189. A Pompeian inscription of the year 13 showing back-slanted kinesthetic tendency. Naples, National Museum.

193

THE 'L' STROKE AND ROUNDED BOTTOM JUNCTURES IN B, D, E, AND L

Actually the 'L' stroke is a stem with a long edge-out stroke, that is, right foot-serif. But a fillet connects stems and serifs. Consequently the bottom join of stem and arm in B, D, E, and L, is in fact a fillet, hence rounded like one, whereas upper junctures of B, D, and E are the normal junctures of separate letter parts, hence angular.

THE NUMERAL MARK

The Romans used letters for their numerals, distinguishing them by putting a "number mark" over any letter to be read as a number. This mark is identical in structure with the arm of T, differing only in length. It consists of a horizontal stroke connecting a left and right arm-serif. In the Trajan Inscription there are three of these marks, two over VI's and the third (ten inches long) over the number XVII.

Fig. 190. Brush-written Roman numeral XIV.

194

Among the letters there is but one, T, which has a left arm-serif, whereas several, C, E, F, G, L, and T, have right arm-serifs. Making left and right arm-serifs, pointed in different directions, in the same stroke seems contradictory. The isolated example of one letter (T) with left

Fig. 191. The numeral mark, or arm of T.

Fig. 192. Roman numeral 2 taken from a first century Vatican Gallery inscription.

195

arm-serif may be the reason its making seems contrary and unnatural. However from the viewpoint of structure the left serif is not unique. It is likened to serifs beginning vertical stems, the difference being that the left serif begins the horizontal arm. The secret to making the arm of T and the numeral mark is that the edge-in stroke shaping the left serif has a cant of about 85 degrees. As soon as this edge-in stroke is begun the brush is immediately twirled into the normal 25-30 degrees cant. The stroke ends with the usual brush twirl shaping the fillet and right arm-serif, which points down and out at about 90 degrees. Figure 192 shows numeral 2 taken from a first century Vatican Lapidary Gallery inscription. The brush origin of the numeral mark is clearly evident.

Here it is pertinent to point out that shaded, Roman reed writing came before square-edged brush writing, that the chisel-shaped writing brush is the gifted, sophisticated child of the square-edged reed, and is

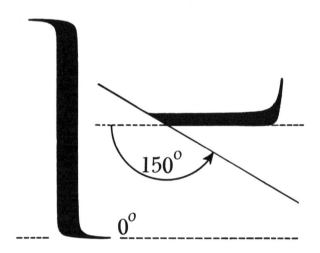

Fig. 193. The cant-latitude (150 degrees) between vertical stems and horizontal bottom arms of C, E, and L.

•

able to perform tasks beyond the capability of its parent, the reed. For example, inscription letters may be brush written comfortably with cants varying from zero to 70 or more degrees—as the numeral mark

196

shows. The fact that the edge-in stroke of classic, monumental letters can vary as much as 150 degrees supports this observation (Cf. figs. 191, 192, 193, and 203). But, in the Republic, the Roman reading public was conditioned to a pattern of visual expectancy by the characteristic and traditional reed-writing cant of 25-30 degrees—which carried over into monumental inscription writing. This fact appears as additional confirmation of earlier observations (chaps. 17 and 18) that formal brush writing (and hence, classic lapidary letters,) came after, not before, Roman reed writing.

•

The Inner-Foot serif of Thick Obliques

In chapter seven some Trajan foot-serifs, for example, A, I, M, P, and X, because they were not perpendicular to the vertical stem, were used as one objection to the "chisel" theory. In the light of our knowl-

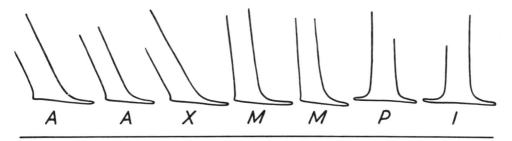

A   A   X   M   M   P   I

Fig. 194. Trajan letters with inclined base serifs.

•

edge of brush handling it is now apparent that these base serifs are the normal, down-and-out, edge-out, brush stroke — perhaps even influencing, or being influenced by the 'L' stroke. The right foot-serif is basic to stems while the left is more or less adventitious. Without question long experience in brush writing with its kinesthetic anticipation and "follow-through" accent of the bottom edge-out stroke tends unconsciously to increase this serif's size and length. Figure 195 shows

197

Fig. 195. Brush-written stem bases.

some brush-written, serifed, stem bases illustrating this down-and-out proneness. Some thick obliques, notably A, M, and X, do not have clearly defined left foot-serifs on the base. Figure 196 shows some of these base serifs and for practical purposes the left foot-serif is absent. Some readers, influenced by a recent author who denigrated the Trajan

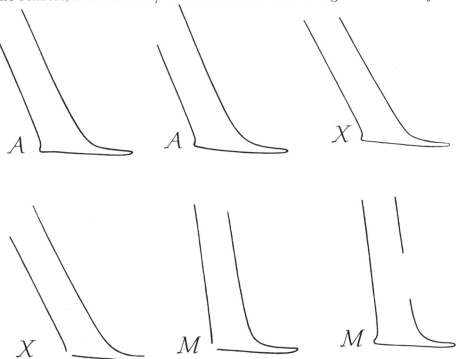

Fig. 196. Some Trajan A, M, and X base serifs.

198

letters saying they were decadent and spuriously contrived, might conclude that such A, M, and X base serifs were unique to the Trajan Inscription, and not the natural result of brush dynamics. Actually such foot-serifs were a common, over-all tradition for at least a century before the Trajan Inscription was written and cut. Figure 197 shows A and M

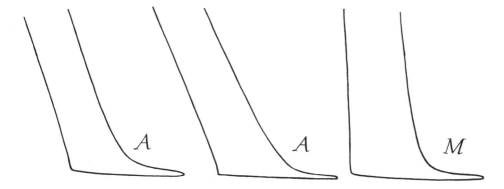

Fig. 197. Augustan letters ten and eleven inches tall, the one on the left from an inscription in the Naples National Museum, the other two from a Roman Forum inscription.

•

serifs from some large and beautiful Augustan letters cut at the end of the first century B.C. (Cf. Fig. 163). The shape of these base serifs and those ending Trajan thick obliques poses no problem for it is the natural, single, edge-out stroke of the brush, whereas the lack of an inner foot-serif on these thick obliques demands an explanation.

The absence of a left foot-serif on vertical stems would be awkward and ugly. Not so a lack of the inner foot-serif on the slanting, thick oblique of A, M, and X. The thick oblique of these letters is a full brush-width stroke, therefore slightly wider than upright stems. Since the oblique intersects the baseline at an angle the wide intersection and terminal serif are as broad as normal base serifs in other letters. But to add an inner, left foot-serif to this broad base and edge-out stroke, would result in a wide base wholly disproportionate in relation to normal base

199

serifs. Consequently to preserve the over-all relationship of top and bottom bases, the inner foot-serif is omitted from the thick oblique of A, M, and X. Figure 198 shows the normal base serif for letter A, and a stem serif for **P** (diagrams *a* and *b*). Diagram *c* shows an inner foot-serif added to A's thick oblique.

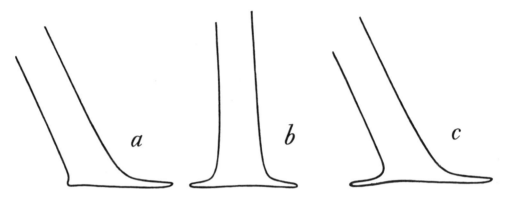

Fig. 198. Normal base serifs of A and a vertical stem (P), and a thick oblique of letter A with an added inner foot-serif.

•

On the other hand, thin obliques in letters A, M, and X, need inner foot-serifs in order to relate with normal basal widths. Moreover in the interest of ease in reading one could suppose, but not prove, that the lack of left foot-serifs from thick obliques in these letters aids visual momentum, and 'moves' the reader on to the next letter. In general though, inner foot-serifs, where used, are shorter than their companion outer serifs. Head serifs of V and X show a like treatment. This is more readily grasped inasmuch as outer head-serifs on V and X are the basic edge-in strokes of these long obliques, hence, when written, kinesthetically emphasized over the inner, head-serifs. Figure 200 shows letters V and X with long outer and short inner head-serifs from a first century inscription now in the Vatican. Figure 201 shows a letter Y from a Pompeian inscription, written and cut in 2 B.C. This letter, 6-1/2 inches tall and now in Naples National Museum, demonstrates clearly that the outer

200

head-serifs are the natural, brush, edge-in stroke for Y's obliques—as
well as for the obliques of X and V.

Fig. 199. Brush strokes in letter V and X.

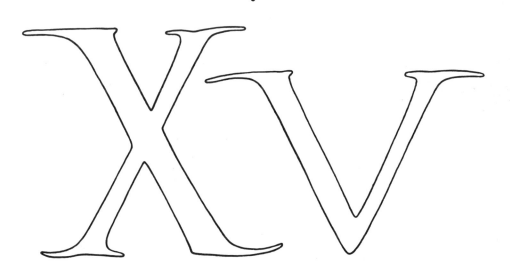

*Fig. 200. Long outer and short inner head-serifs of letters X and V
taken from a first century inscription. (¾). Vatican Lapidary Galleries*

201

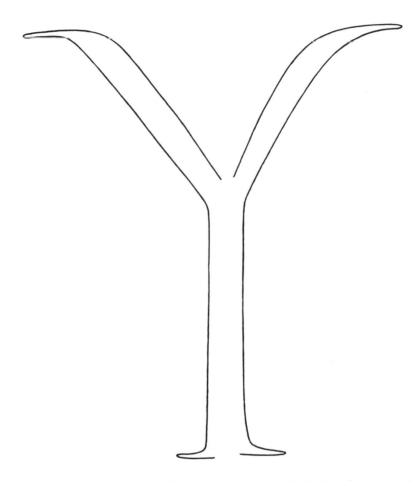

Fig. 201. An incised letter Y from Pompeii (2 B.C.) showing the normal, edge-in, brush stroke for the two obliques. Naples National Museum. (2/3).

•

ROUNDED JUNCTURES AND ARMS

In chapter seven one of many objections to the "chisel" theory for the origin of the serif was that fact that some Imperial letters (A, C, E, G, L, M, S, and V) had letter parts whose endings were neither square, angled, nor serifed. Instead these parts are blunt and rounded, directly contradicting authors who say that the 'chisel when cutting letters pre-

202

fers angled, squared, and serifed ends.' Round stroke endings are found in the oblique junctures of A, M, N, and V, and the bottom arm of C, E, G, L, and S. They are the result of normal brush handling as the

Fig. 202. *Rounded obliques and arm endings.*

A   *M*   *N*   *V*

Fig. 203. *The single strokes that fashion round ends of letters A, M, N, and V.*

C G   S   E L

Fig. 203a. The single strokes that fashion round ends of letters C, G,. S, E, and L.

•

strokes in figure 203 demonstrate. Note that outer top oblique junctures are smaller than corresponding bottom junctures in letters M and N. The brush begins the top edge-in stroke quickly and edges-out at the bottom slowly. This accounts for the variance in these top and bottom junctures. The top juncture of letter A and the bottom of V also follow this rule.

•

THE FOOT SERIF OF THICK OBLIQUES IN A, M, AND X

When the basic brush strokes which produce the obliques of A, M, and X are compared with other letters having similar brush dynamics a seeming contradiction turns up. As indicated above there is little or no inner foot-serif on the thick strokes of letters A, M, and X in the Trajan Inscription. Instead this spot on the left foot is either angled or has a barely perceptible 'serif' as figures 196 and 197 show. Yet in the Trajan Inscription oblique junctures of A, M, N, V, and the bottom arm-ends of C, E, G, L, and S are always rounded (Fig. 202), and, in making the thick obliques of A, X, and M, the brush usually makes a round corner as it edges-out into the right foot serif. Figure 203 shows these brush strokes with rounded corners. What is the reason for the differing treatment of a similarly written letter part? One explanation for this angled corner of A, M, and X is that the thick oblique converging into the horizontal baseline initiates a forceful visual momentum which must be checked, otherwise a visual momentum 'skid' below the base-

204

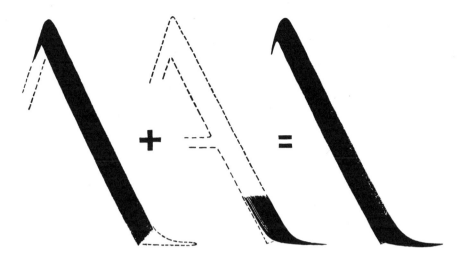

Fig. 204. The thick oblique of A, M, and X made in two strokes.

•

line may result[24]. A sharp corner at this spot with a crisp change of direction seems to check this visual slippage.

There is another explanation which, however requires that the thick oblique in A, M, and X be made in two strokes rather than one. Figure 204 illustrates such a two-stroke oblique for letters A, M, and X.

•

FLAT AND POINTED TOPS IN A, M, AND N

Today we are conditioned in our reading by roman type capitals whose straight letters have flat tops. Three Trajan capitals, A, M, and

Fig. 205. Pointed tops in Trajan letters.

205

N, are angled. In lecture-demonstrations on Trajan letters my experience is that audiences accept the main features of the letter-shape and serif-origin thesis as being the product of the brush but question the thesis because of these angled tops. In fact these three letters have been used by some writers to prove that the Trajan letter is actually a decadent retrogression of an earlier, more vigorous letter shape. These writers further insist that early, first century majuscules with flat tops are better models for present-day study and imitation.

•

. . . the upper (flat) limitation in the A, M, and N, as done exclusively in the first half of the first century, is replaced by a point which cannot be made by writing.

Walter Kaeck, *Rhythm and Proportion in Lettering,* p. 37.

•

This statement and others like it presume that the 'decadent' pointed top was an invention of the Trajan master or of another calli-

Fig. 206. Angled tops and bottoms in Trajan letters.

grapher in the late first or early second century, and that the flat top ceased after the first half of the first century. The truth is, as any paleographer knows, angled tops were made in the first century B.C. — for example, the magnificent, eleven-inch tall, Augustan letters (Fig. 163) on public view in the Roman Forum — and, furthermore, flat tops to A, M, and N (Cf. Fig. 215) were written after the first half of the first century.

It is evident that a prejudice exists against angled tops by the fact that no one complains about angled bottoms of G, M, N, and V, which existed alongside flat and top-pointed letters throughout the Imperium and, centuries later, were cut by type founders. Though reasons are not given I suspect several factors underlie this prejudice against pointed tops such as: 1) since most A, M, and N, typeface capitals have flat tops, we have become accustomed to reading these caps and anything at odds with our reading habits is difficult to accept; 2) pointed tops to A, M, and N cannot be made with the reed-pen or the 2-pencil marking device which, some contend, were the tools that originally shaped Latin letters; 3) ignorance of the square-edged brush and its handling.

Fig. 207. Pointed and flat tops in inscription A.

207

There is a justification, however, for pointed Imperial A, M, and N. Contrary to accepted belief, pointed tops can be brush-written in one stroke (Fig. 203) by changing cant during stroking, though it requires advanced skill. In addition the angled top in inscription cutting has the merit of simplicity (one in place of two corners) and economy, basics of formal *scriptura monumentalis*. It saves cutting time for it eliminates a corner. (Fig. 207). Finally the pointed top undoubtedly was the attempt by the Imperial writing masters to fix a relationship and unity among top junctures of A, M, and N and pointed, bottom junctures of G, M, N, and V. It is a truism that simplicity, economy, and unity are essentials of genuine art.

•

IMPERIAL LETTER N WITH THICK STEMS

Another Imperial letter which provokes comment, though not so often as the pointed A, M, and N, is Trajan N with its two thick stems and one thick oblique stroke. One reason why this is not more widely known is doubtless the misleading reproductions of 'Trajan' letters drawn by authors and designers for their calligraphy manuals and lettering books (Cf. Fig. 228). These authors redesign Trajan N so that it has thinner stems to contrast with the thick oblique, thus conforming to what we are led to expect, typographically, in modern N's.

Fig. 208. Modern typographic N's with thin stems.

•

In contrast, figure 209 shows three letters taken from an inscription cut in the year 75 and now in the Vatican Lapidary Galleries. The stems of this N, like Trajan N's, are almost equal in width to regular stems of other letters and these, combined with the thick oblique, in effect

208

produce an N having three thick and no thin strokes. This, of course, is unacceptable in roman typeface design today and proves to what extent we are conditioned to a pattern of reading expectancy which, since the 15th century, has given us two hairline, thin stems for letter N.

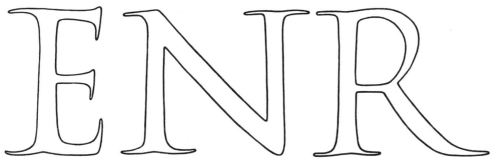

Fig. 209. First century Roman letters from an inscription in the Vatican Lapidary Galleries in which letter N has three thick strokes (½).

•

On the other hand Imperial sign writers and inscription makers had no printing tradition to respect or to restrain them. They created *ex novo*. Their letter flowed naturally from their tool, the flat, chisel-shaped brush, and, inasmuch as the Imperial N had two vertical stems, there was no reason to make them differ from other vertical stems.

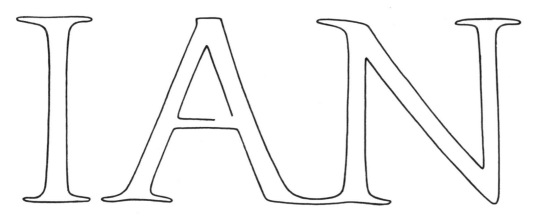

Fig. 210. Letters IAN from a Puteoli inscription of the year 92. National Museum, Naples.

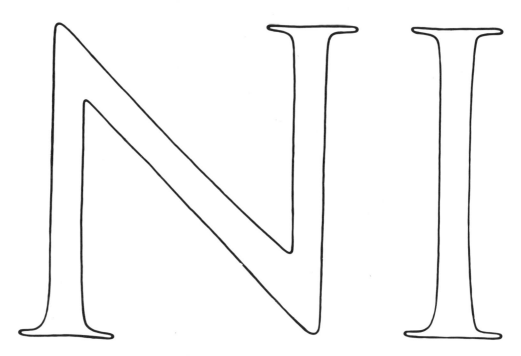

Fig. 211. Letters NI from a well-designed, first century Imperial inscription. (4/5). National Museum, Ravenna.

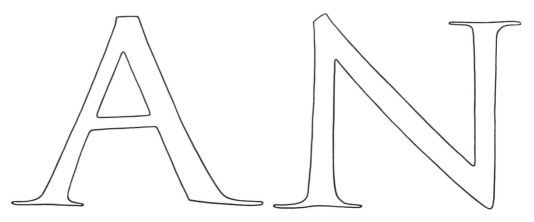

Fig. 212. Letters AN from an Ostian inscription of the year 75. (1/2). Vatican Lapidary Galleries.

210

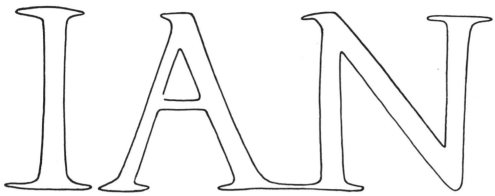

Fig. 213. Letters IAN from an inscription (c.a.64) in the Naples National Museum. (4/5).

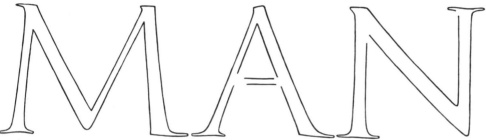

Fig. 214. Letters MAN from an inscription made during the reign of Emperor Caligula (37-41). (1/2). Palazzo di Drago, Rome.

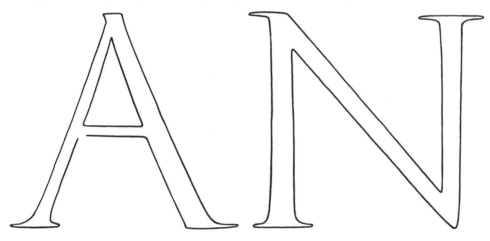

Fig. 215. Letters AN from a Hadrianic inscription in Puteoli. (3/5). National Museum, Naples.

One is not to conclude, however, that all Roman N's had only thick stems. Half- and three-quarters-thick stems were common throughout the Imperium. Thin-stemmed N's were usually found in semi-formal and informal cursive inscriptions whereas full-stemmed N's more often were associated with carefully made, formal, monumental letters. One explanation is that semi-formal script is more compact and condensed than formal script thus permitting more semi-formal letters to be written in a given space. Moreover, one, using normal, Roman cant. finds it easier to brush-write a thin vertical than a thin, left-to-right oblique stroke. Hence the tendency in semi-formal brush writing to favor thin-stemmed, narrow N's. In addition a narrow N with three thick strokes would be calligraphically absurd. In compensation monumental N's are quite wide in order to accommodate the three thick strokes. Figures 209 through 215 show formal, thick-stemmed monumental N's taken from various Imperial inscriptions of which **six** are from the first century and one from the first quarter of the second century.

29

Interaction of brush & chisel

ne is not to assume that the letterer, in the act of chiselling the inscription, blindly followed every mark, ec-
centricity, or fault of spontaneous writing. The inscription maker began as a writer when wielding the
brush, became a letterer when chiselling, and ended as a sign painter
when painting or gilding the chiselled V-cut letters.

But as a letterer, cutting the letters, he corrected whatever writing
mistakes, wavering brush strokes, and incorrect relationships had occurred in the original writing. He started his brush writing with a predetermined formal exemplar in his mind, an exemplar based entirely
on brush manipulation. If some parts of his written letters did not measure up to the mental pattern the *same formal exemplar* continued to
dictate to him when he was in the lettering (cutting) phase of the inscription sequence, not unlike the skilled sign man who makes a quick,
single-line layout over which he paints finished letters.

Such a stone letterer, like the sound craftsman in any craft, would
understand the limitations of his tools and materials. He avoids deep
V-cuts because of the increased danger of edge-fracture; and for the same
reason he avoids sharp, stone junctures and internally projecting points
of stone.

In brush writing an internal projection often occurs at the juncture
of stem and upper arm in letters such as B, D, E, F, P, and R. If, in
chiselling these letter parts, the cutter should cut slavishly only what
had been written, the resultant letter would have internally projecting
points which invite breakage. The experienced letterer removes these
'negative' projections. Then too some brush strokes project over other
strokes, for example, R's mid-arm in figure 216 which starts at the left of

213

the stem and extends beyond the lobe. The calligrapher-chiseller ignores
these when cutting.

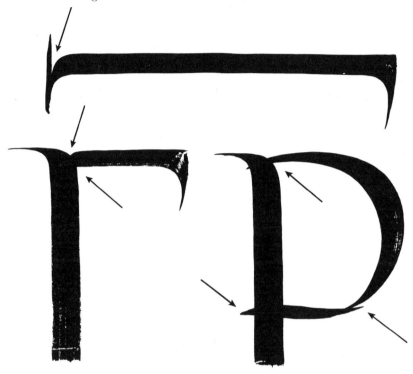

Fig. 216. Brush-written internal and external projections.

214

30

How inscription was written

ow was the brush held in writing ancient inscriptions? Three methods are possible and each leads to the same end—Imperial majuscules. The first is the show card writing technique (method "1") in which the brush writer holds the brush almost upright and rests the outer side of his palm on the writing surface. This palm - and - hand position, acceptable for very smooth surfaces as cloth, cardboard, paper, etc., could not be sustained

Fig. 217. Show-card writing position. Method "1."

•

long on rough surfaces like unpolished marble or stuccoed walls. It is chiefly an indoor technique for smaller work laid flat or inclined slightly. Its use is awkward for vertical signs, windows, walls, or large letters.

The second method ("2"), is the *sign painter's* usual manner. It is one in which the writer rests his brush hand on the mahl stick held in his left hand. This method is a bit slower than the show-card discipline but it has the advantage of greater control, added finesse, and it permits

215

Fig. 218. Sign painter using mahl stick in writing and lettering signs, Method "2".

•

the writer to work over previously painted but wet letters — a course not possible or at least difficult in method "1". It is also the preferred and natural position for writing signs on the job.

The third method ("3"), most difficult of all, is that in which the writer holds the brush at the tip of the handle and twirls the brush to effect changes in cant. This is somewhat akin to the system adopted by sign men when painting upright, highway bulletins and huge wall signs. However, their tool usually is a long-handled "fitch," a specially shaped, hog-bristle brush.

I have lectured on the origin of the serif before the Society of Typographic Arts in Chicago in 1956; at the Portland, Oregon, Art Museum in 1958; at the Rockefeller Institute in New York in 1962; at Reed College in 1963, and at the Los Angeles County Museum of Art in 1966. In all these lectures I have demonstrated method "3", writing capitals

216

*Fig. 219. Sign man writing wall in-
scriptions with the brush held at
the tip of the handle. Method "3".*

•

eight to ten inches tall on a vertical board, and using a no. 16 or no. 18
red sable, flat, "brights" brush. An alphabet of demonstration letters on
paper written for a lecture at the "Third Festival of Art and Worship"
at Norwich, Vermont, in 1963 is now preserved in the Houghton Library
at Harvard, and others like it at the Portland Museum and the Los Angeles County Museum of Art to accompany the three alphabet stones
the museums bought for their permanent collections.

Method "1" would be acceptable for smooth stones laid flat or
slightly tilted, and one would suppose that small stones in ancient Rome
were made in this manner. If we are to believe ancient advertisements,
the Roman sign man in his shop wrote, cut, and finished small inscrip-

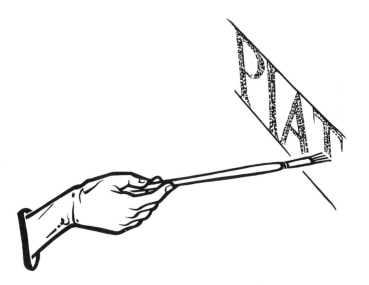

Fig. 220. Close-up view of figure 206, method "3".

•

tions which then were installed by the client much like today's signs, made indoors to be located elsewhere. Without doubt most large inscriptions in antiquity were written and cut on the job much as delicate architectural detail was finished, in place rather than at the quarry or shop. Hence methods "2" or "3" were used for large work outdoors and on the job with method "2" perhaps the more common. But for extremely large letters like the ten-inch Augustan letters in the Naples Museum and the eleven-inch Augustan letters (Fig. 163) in the Roman Forum, method "3" is more likely to have been used.

Some of the basic strokes of Imperial letters are shown in figures 222, 223, and 224. These elements, including all their cant variations and changes, are directly written in one stroke. They have not been retouched or retraced. From these elements one can make *every letter* shape and part of the best Imperial lettering, including, of course, their serifs, and if needed, even reversed (boustrophedon) letters, though, with less facility by right-handed writers. Each stroke is placed at about the same height as it would have were it a part of an actual letter. Thus

218

one can distinguish the arms and serifs of C, E, L, S; the lobe of R; and some obliques of A, M, and V.

Fig. 221. The author demonstrating brush writing method no. "3" and making Imperial capital letters with their serifs for an audience at the Rockefeller Institute, New York City, June 25, 1960. On the poster paper taped to the black board one can recognize some of the topics discussed, e.g., brush-written inter-points, arm serifs, various capital letters, edging-in and -out, and deep versus shallow V-cutting in stone. Photo courtesy of A. Burton Carnes, New York.

219

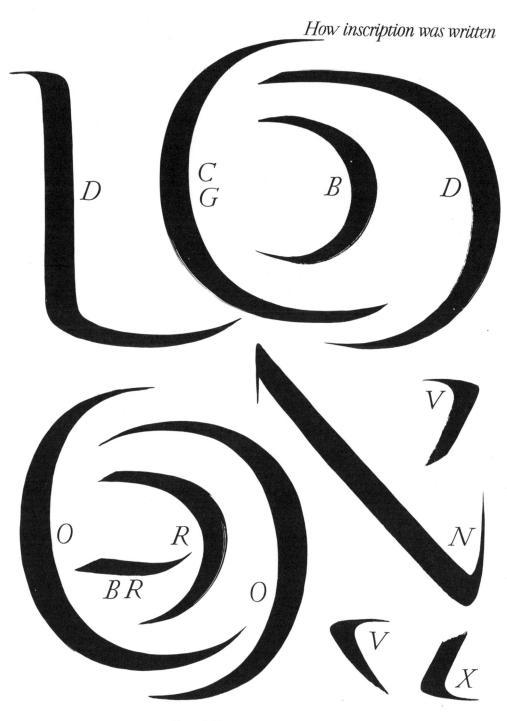

Fig. 222. Basic brush strokes.

Fig. 223. Basic brush strokes.

Fig. 224. Basic brush strokes.

222

31

The letters arranged

ow that a reasonable support has been fixed for the brush
origin of Roman letters and their serifs, and, in the process, some misconceptions righted, can we crown our task
by putting our findings to work? That is, can one write
out Imperial majuscules complete in all their parts, their
characteristic swells, bows, lobes, fillets, serifs, tails, cant changes, stems,
arms, strokes sequences and directions, and do it in an integrated, *consistently repeated* brush-writing technique? The answer is yes. The following 38 letters, numeral mark, and inter-point are offered in demonstration.

The letters printed in burnt siena are the letter standard (redrawn
from rubbings and squeezes of the Trajan Inscription in Rome) against
which our brush-written demonstration letters, printed in green, are
tested and compared. The Trajan letters are of the same height and
mostly from the Inscription's second and third lines, which contain the
tallest letters. Not all the letters of the alphabet occur in these lines, but
those that do not have been reproportioned to this height. The stem of
F in the Trajan Inscription is slightly thicker than stems of other letters
of the same height. This stem has been reshaped to fit the remaining
letters.

Each letter part of the green demonstration letters, bow, stem, arm,
tail, etc., is *written* in a predetermined stroke sequence and direction.
There is no retouching or retracing of strokes to improve letters. To
avoid suspicion, these letters have been purposely written in dry brush
technique. Therefore brush streaks are intentional as partial proof
against retouching or retracing over strokes. The length of Q's tail presented problems. In order to show Q vertically as other letters are shown,

it would have been necessary either 1) to bind in a folded page insert, 2) to print Q's tail in two parts on one page or 3) to print it on both pages across the book's hinge. The method chosen, in which the Q's are turned ninety degrees counterclockwise, seemed best for comparing the letters. Each green and burnt siena letter has its own page excepting letter I, the inter-point, and the numeral mark, which, in order to conserve space, are grouped together on one page.

In letters where basic strokes join each other at angles, and particularly where these angles are acute, as in A, M, and N, the secondary edge-in and edge-out strokes are normally concealed by overlapping. I have purposely shortened some strokes in order to show how these junctures are actually made. (Fig. 225).

Fig. 225. Basic strokes purposely shortened to show their edge-in and edge-out cant angles.

•

For those who may wish to write their own inscription letters, figure 226 shows the essential strokes for some letters of the classic inscription alphabet. Figure 227 shows such a brush-written inscription.

Fig. 226. Basic strokes for some letters of the inscription alphabet.

225

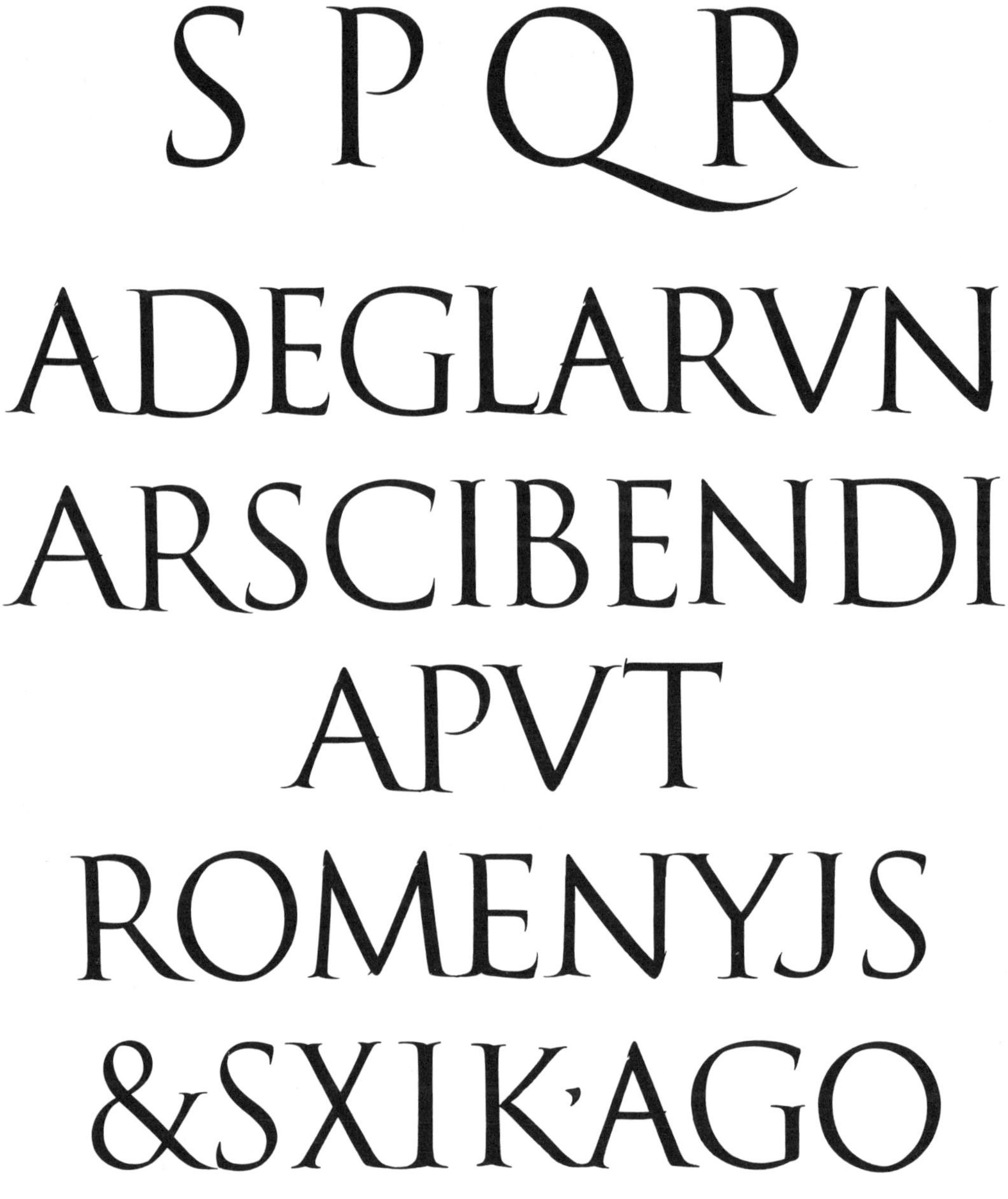

S P Q R

ADEGLARVN

ARSCIBENDI

APVT

ROMENYJS

&SXI K·AGO

Fig. 227. A brush-written, inscription layout preparatory to chiselling.

The letters compared

n the following pages the basic, freely-written *scriptura monumentalis,* printed in green, is shown on the left. Each letter is faced on the right with its like though finished letter (actually redrawn Trajan letters), printed in burnt siena.

228

229

230

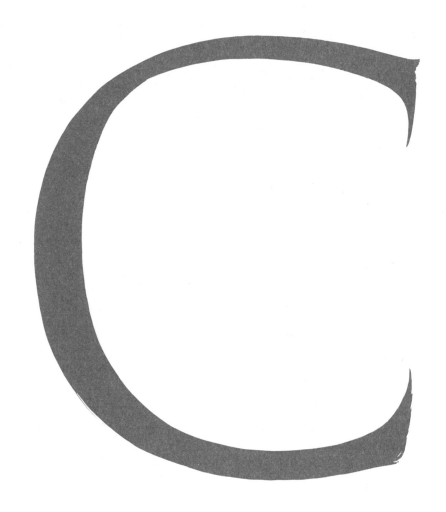

232

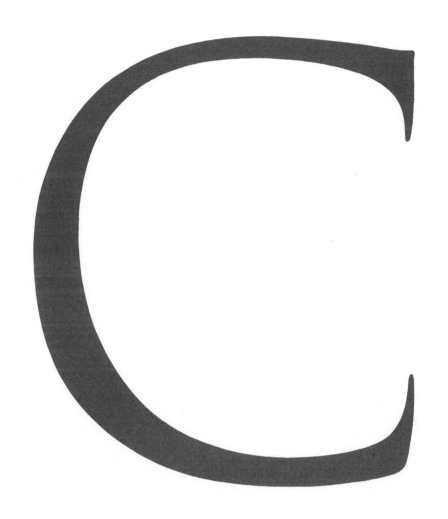

233

234

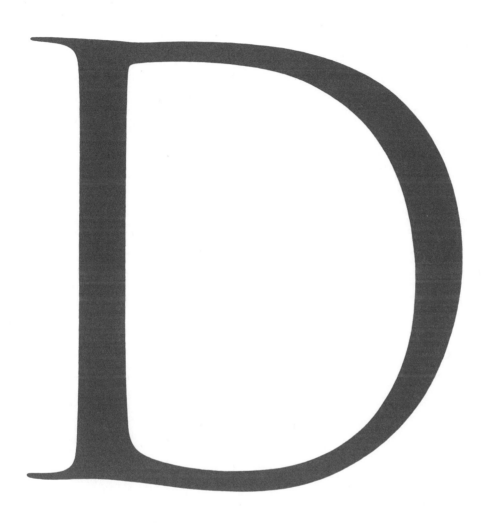

235

236

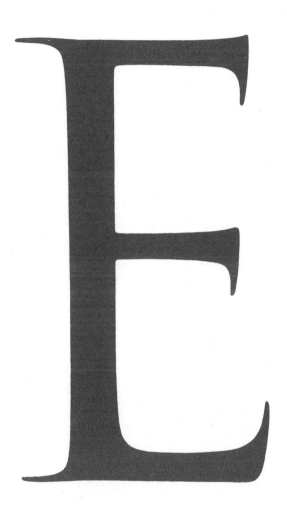

238

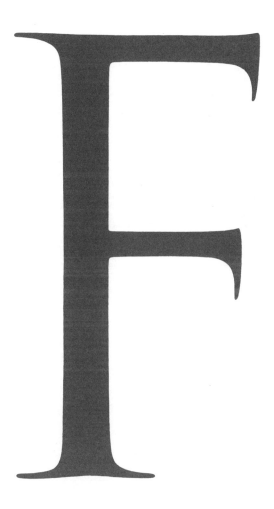

239

240

241

242

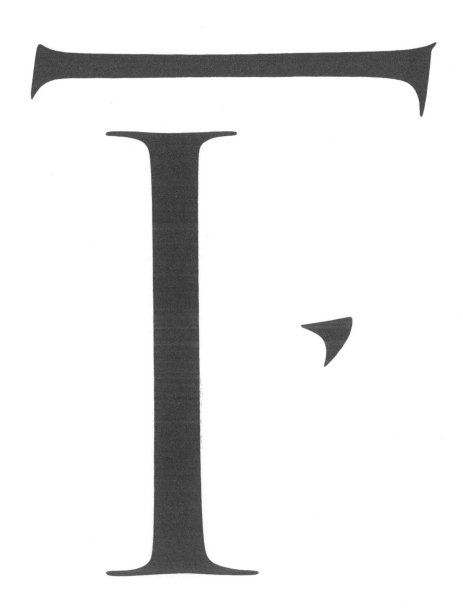

243

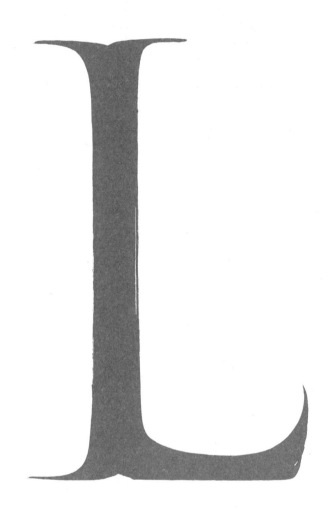

244

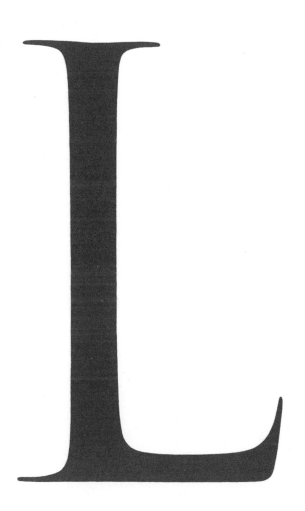

246

247

248

249

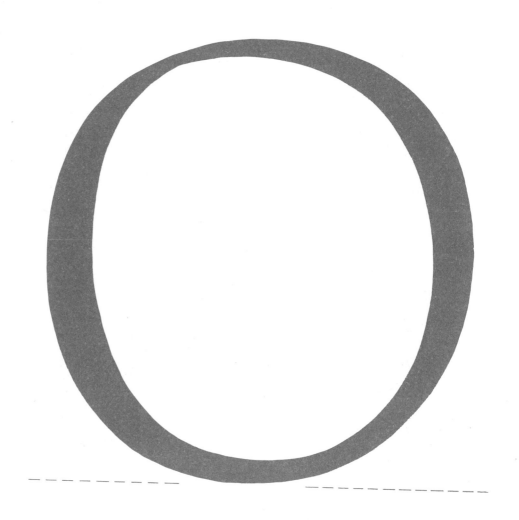

250

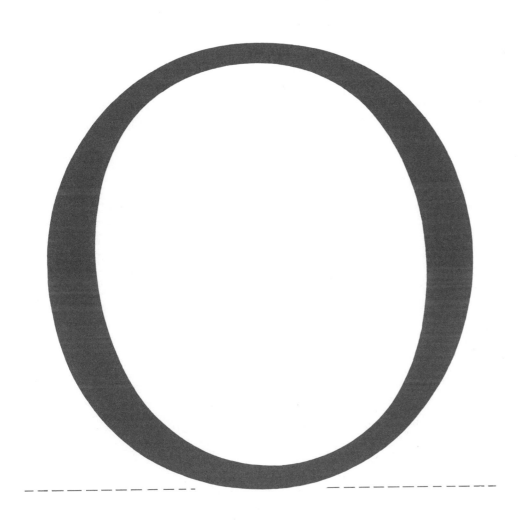

251

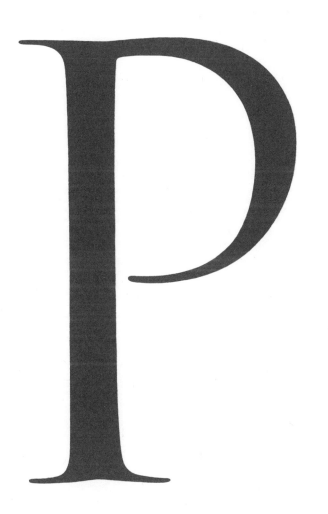

253

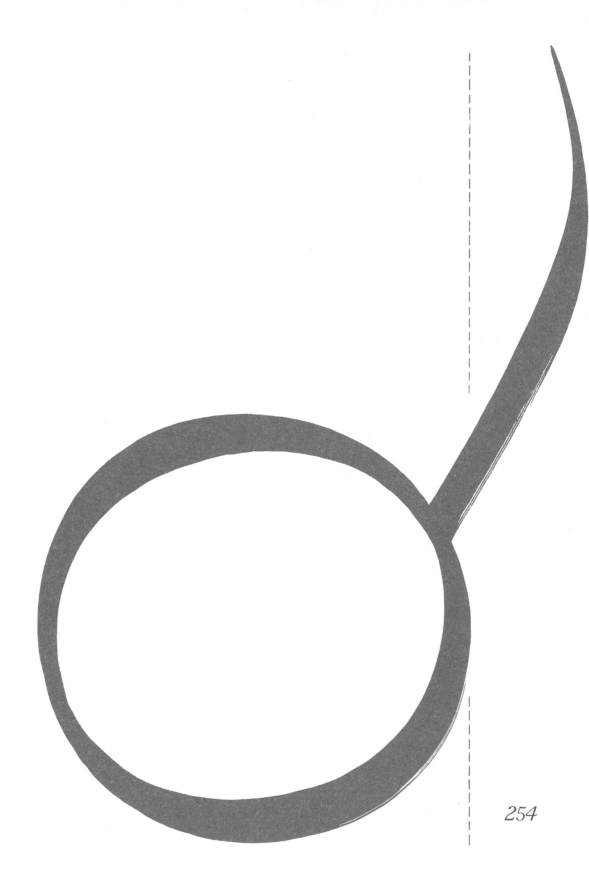

254

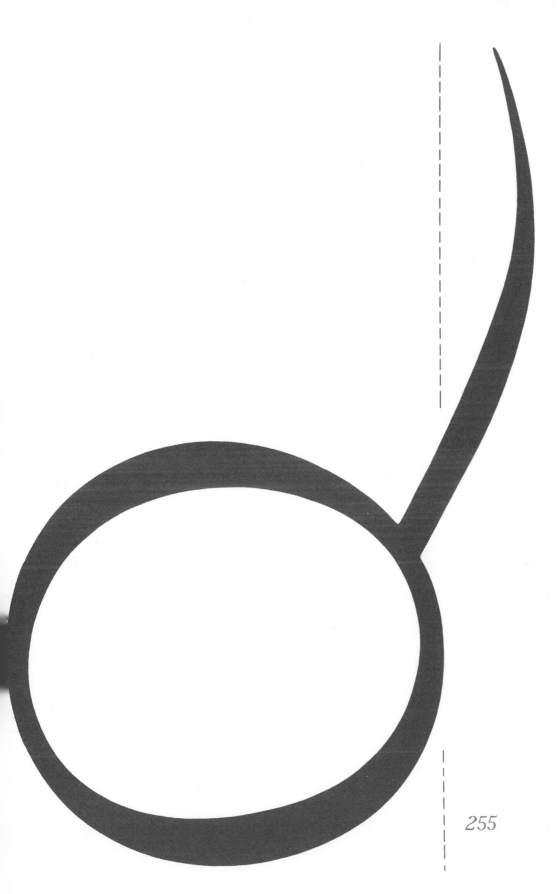

255

256

258

260

261

262

263

264

Calligraphic unity in Rome

sually readers are curious to learn the genesis of any new approach to an old problem, particularly if that approach contradicts or questions accepted opinion. In this book on the origin of the serif I do not claim any unique, intuitive insight. I am sure that, once my suggestions are clearly stated, any present-day sign writer will readily accept them. But why has not this thesis been proposed before?

There seem to be several reasons. Foremost is the fact that true brush writing of roman letters has been almost non-existent since the Roman Empire and was reborn at about the turn of the century in our country; secondly, sign and show-card writers in our times have *never been aware* that they shared their craft with Imperial inscription makers. Again, our thinking about roman majuscules has been confused and obscured by ideas of geometric and mechanical letter construction, introduced in the Renaissance by Felice Feliciano and followed by a host of disciples. Furthermore, theorizing about the origins of ancient letters has been done by paleographers, typographers, letterers, and hard-tool calligraphers and not by brush-wielding sign writers. Finally a failure to see *writing as the source* of all other kinds of graphic expression has blinded us to the logical relationships that exist amongst them.

For example, Figure 228 shows Trajan letters as they are and as they have been represented. The top row shows letters carefully redrawn from tracings of rubbings and squeezes taken from the original Inscription in Rome; the middle and bottom rows show the same letters photographed from those presented by two authorities on lettering, (one a noted typographer, the other a commercial letterer), in books published in 1936 and 1961 respectively. The 1936 book, written by the typogra-

AMNPR
AMNPR
AMNPR

Fig. 228. Trajan letters as they are (top row) and as they have been represented by a typographer (middle row) and a commercial letterer (bottom row).

•

pher, is devoted solely to the Trajan Inscription alphabet. It contains drawings of Trajan letters each of which shows forth the typographic thinking of its author. The 1961 book authored by the commercial letterer contains a Trajan alphabet intended as an inspirational model for students and calligraphers. Like the typographic 'Trajan' alphabet, this book contains Trajan letters as interpreted by one who makes letters by outlining and filling-in. The middle row of figure 228 shows some of the typographic 'Trajan' letters and the bottom row some of the letterer's 'Trajan' letters. Except for N and R the general proportions of the copies are close to the originals, but there the accuracy stops. In the middle row notice especially the added foot serifs in A and M, the sharpening and dropping of lower points of M and N, the tilting of the bar of A, curving of right leg of M, enlarging of the lobe of P, alterna-

267

tion of tail of R, and the general typographic blobbiness of the serifs. In the bottom row notice many of the same inaccuracies plus exaggerated thinness of thin strokes, especially in A, M, and N, the upward turn of the lobe P, and spikey rather than treacly serifs. These interpretations, which do not exhaust the list of re-designed 'Trajan' alphabets, point up the printing-lettering mentality inherited from the Renaissance and how distantly removed we are from the writing orientation in the making of letters.

It is my good fortune to have been a professional sign writer before studying Roman archeology, epigraphy and paleography. While doing epigraphic research in Italy during the years 1935-39 I saw numerous Imperial inscriptions which showed unmistakedly the basic characteristics and kinesthetics of brush writing familiar to me as a Chicago sign writer. In the twentieth century such a combination of archeologist, stone-cutter and commercial sign writer is extremely unlikely to coincide in one person; whereas in old Rome professional competence in writing with both pen and brush and chiselling signs was a normal and natural combination.

We live in an age of specialization. More and more our productive activities tend to be departmentalized. No man can be an expert in all the techniques by which these departments are served, and it is difficult, almost to the point of impossibility, to see the wilderness of subdivisions as a whole. We calligraphers suffer from these general disabilities, and tend to project into our view of the past our own limitations. Thus there arises the danger, when writing about ancient letter making, of concluding that Roman calligraphers, were, like us, one-sided specialists.

But in antiquity the calligrapher's art was practiced as a compact unified whole. The cutting of letters was not a specialized accomplishment set apart from the rest of letter making. Emil Hübner states that in the Palermo Museum there is an inscription in Greek and Latin advertising the work of a professional calligrapher, "tituli heic ordinantur et sculpuntur..." (Op. Cit. p. xxx.) that is, "signs written and cut here." And there is a Roman inscription very much like it, "... titulos scribendos vel si quid marmorarii opus fuerit hic habes ..." meaning, "marble

268

work and sign writing here."

The letter cutter was a journeyman sign writer who could write his inscription and also cut it. The Latin verb *incido, cisi, cisum*, meant not only to cut in, to carve, and engrave, but to inscribe. "Id non modo tum scripserunt, verum etiam in aere incisum nobis tradiderunt." "Not only did they record it in writing, but they presented it to us inscribed in bronze." (Cicero, *Actio in Verrem*, 2, 4, 65).

In 1936 in the cortile of the Naples Museum I saw an unfinished Pompeian, Rustic inscription of four lines in which the last several letters of the fourth line had not been cut. I could see faint traces of red in the letters still to be cut and no trace of color in the cut letters. The thought that immediately came to mind was that it could possibly have been a quadrator's bit of work interrupted by the Vesuvian eruption of 79 A.D. In 1950 and again in 1955 and 1960 I made exhaustive search for this small marble slab, in order to make photographs, rubbings and squeezes of it, but to no avail. It was not listed in the Museum inventory and none of the Museum personnel whom I consulted recalled it. In the Museum of Pavia there is a chiselled inscription containing five lines (C.I.L. III 6421), in which the last two lines are written in red, not carved.

Furthermore the Latin word *scribo* meant 'to engrave,' 'to scratch,' 'chisel letters,' as well as 'to write.' Hübner, whose erudition was unusually deep, tells us that 'writing stood for either or both processes of layout and chiselling' : "Scribendi igitur vocabulum quamquam per se utrumque significat compositionem et scalpturam, . ." (Ibid., p. xxvi.) The Hebrew word *Katab* means 'to write' and 'to incise.'

Has there ever been an inscription making craft like Rome's from which we could derive information about craft methods and practices, which in turn could help us understand Rome's inscription making methods? One that quite possibly could help is the tomb writing and cutting craft during the Han Dynasties (Western 206 B.C., to A.D. 25; Eastern, 25-200 A.D.) —co-existing roughly with Imperial Rome's craft. Unfortunately, we have no Han documentation, from which we could extract technical secrets and practices.

Some writers, in both calligraphy and iconography, state that classic inscription technique was resurrected in the Renaissance. It is true that at this time classical inscriptions were rediscovered, collections formed, and decipherment carried on. Letters were admired, copied and used in many contexts, even by the great masters such as Bellini, Mantegna, and Ghirlandaio.

Unhappily the Renaissance craft of stone lettering was unnatural, not vital. It devoted itself to appearances rather than the facts behind the appearances — to effects rather than to causes. Chiselled letters were made following outlining, built-up, and filled-in layout methods. There were even attempts to contrive foolproof geometric formulae for letter making by Fleury, Tory, Moille, Serlio, de' Fanti, Ruano, Dürer, and others— schemes which today are, at most, of interest to typographic researchers and calligraphic historians. These attempts were understandable because free, true, brush writing and its manipulatory mastery were unknown. Had there been a vital practice of brush writing in the Renaissance surely these gifted artist-authors would not have submitted such compass-and-square lettering schemes. A glance at the letters made in the Renaissance shows their unawareness of the internal dynamics of the brush writing that underlay classic lapidary inscriptions.

History thus far is of no help in locating a parallel to Rome's inscription making. Indeed the monumental lettering of our architects has followed the Renaissance error right down to our times. But we have at hand a parallel in the living craft of unpresuming sign writers. Here, working for different purposes, with different materials, and in a completely different culture, the use of the same tools has brought to light truths forgotten for almost eighteen centuries. Chicago sign writers at the beginning of this century have what our architects and other calligraphic designers need to know.

270

34

Craft expressions result from craft technique

Every craft has its technical constants, the ways in which certain materials and tools were repeatedly used establishing technical traditions that are natural, rapid, and appropriate. In every significant artistic accomplishment these technical constants are present as a subordinate though necessary part of the esthetic whole. And it is through these constants that the tools reveal themselves.

For example, coins have been made since classical antiquity yet we have had no coin puncher, hub engraver, or die sinker, of old to explain the art. But if we examine the better coins from Grecian antiquity through Roman, Byzantine, and Medieval eras we discover a similarity in technical achievement despite the different cultural, social, and re-

Fig. 229. Obverse and reverse of Roman, first century coin of Aheno-barbus and contemporary medals of saints in 'dot-dash' coinage.

•

ligious dispositions which colored these ages. Thus we find consistent use of 'dot-dash' coinage. That is in making coin dies, dot and dash punches as chasing tools and punches were frequently used. Truly one

271

could say that in all ages they are the die-sinker's most useful, able in themselves to teach something of their use even to the novice.

In discovering a link between, say, our early twentieth century Chicago sign writers and the Imperial sign writers of the first and second centuries who were their alphabetic progenitors, we need not look for the affinity in external design, the letters created by both. Instead we should search out the craft constants, the tools, technical means, kinesthetics, and craft orientation common to Chicago and Rome. We shall find there is a special reason for citing Chicago and linking it to ancient Rome.

35

Chicago sign writing

In Chicago during the first quarter of this century large department stores employed full time sign and show-card writers who wrote out all the window display cards, show-cards, price tickets, etc. The usual tool for writing was the flat, square, chisel-shaped, red sable brush (sometimes called the "rigger") with which the workman wrote out rapidly, often without guide lines, retouching, or preliminary layout, his signs, cards and tags.

Examples of this manner of brush writing can be claimed for other cities but nowhere was it practiced so widely as to constitute, so to say, a "school" or movement peculiarly its own. We know that Chicago in the 20's was the window trimmer's world capital, and that show-card writing was a vital adjunct to window display art. One of the first large concerns to recognize window dressing as a separate and needed merchandising art was Marshall Field & Co., whose windows even today are among the world's finest.

This brush-writing skill is not to be confused with that of sign painting or sign lettering, in which letters are outlined, worked over, filled-in, and built-up. Fast, direct letter-making, both in department stores and commercial sign shops, was an essential and distinguishing mark of Chicago's sign-making craft. Meticulously and carefully shaped letters, though admired by fellow workmen, often went unnoticed by the sign-shop owner and his client.

The reason for fast letter-production in Chicago at this time is readily understood. Trade unions were strong and wages high. To the sign-shop owner considerations of art and beauty were decidedly secondary to market economics. Accordingly the fast worker who could turn out a commercially acceptable product was highly prized by his wage-

and-price conscious employer, and, in times of stress and unemployment, was the man likely to hold his job.

Let no one think, however, that the resulting commercial sign writing and lettering was mediocre in quality. Eric Gill's statement[25] on sign writing that "Excessive speed in execution—due to 'competition'—has caused a degradation in the form of individual letters" does not bear out the facts in New World practice. The explanation for Chicago's letter-making speed and superior quality is simple.

Forced to work quickly, sign writers soon acquired remarkable skills with various kinds of brushes. One by-product of speed is economy of time and motion. When speed is not essential in brush writing and lettering, a standardized stroke-sequence and -direction might not seem important. But with speed given priority, every slightest saving in time and effort is valued.

For example, until recent times lettering manuals suggested making letter H in the stroke sequence shown on the left[26] in figure 230.

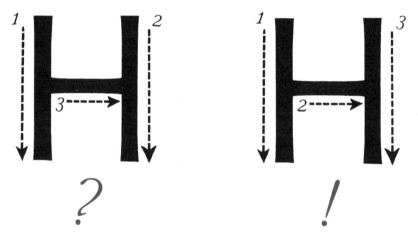

Fig. 230. Wrong and right way for making letter H.

·

The correct way is, however, to make the cross bar as *stroke two* and the right stem as stroke three as on the right in figure 230. In small writing the time saved in making H in the correct stroke-sequence and -direction

274

is negligible. But with large letters of two, three or more inches in height, the time saved would be immediately noticeable. To illustrate, the top row of figure 231 shows two identical H's and a dotted line indi-

Fig. 231. Two identical H's made with differing stroke sequences and directions and the paths followed by the brush in making each letter.

•

cating the invisible path followed by the hand between strokes. In the bottom row the paths followed by the brush both in contact and not in contact with the writing surface are shown as a solid line. It is clear which stroke sequence in making H is quicker and preferable, and which H represents the possibility of smearing over wet strokes.

Figure 232 shows some other stroke sequences and directions. For a complete exposition see *Stroke Sequences and Directions in Writing,* Catholic Art Quarterly, 1946, Pentecost, Vol. 9, no. 3, p. 22.

I am not suggesting that all Chicago sign writers evolved a fixed stroke-sequence and -direction system in their letter making. All I can

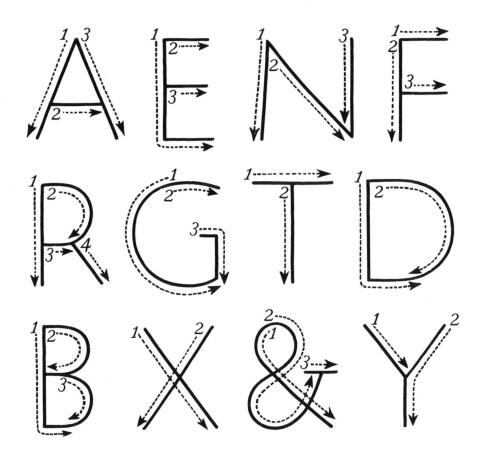

Fig. 232. Some other stroke sequences and directions.

•

report here is that I, as a young apprentice, early formulated for my own use a sequence pattern of strokes for brush writing capitals and small letters.[27] I have had no reason to change these kinesthetic patterns since, even for ordinary, everyday writing with pen and pencil—except for letter F, which later paleographic studies taught me is graphically and kinesthetically related, not to letter E without the bottom arm, but to letter T.

Moreover in building-up compound letters such as *Cooper*,[28] the need for kinesthetic economy suggested strokes like these in figures 233

276

and 234.[29] Ordinarily one would surmise that the stem of letter I, on the right in figure 233 was made first, then the top and bottom serifs; that is, a possibility of two strokes for the stem and two each for head and foot serifs or six strokes in all. As a Chicago writer using the chisel-shaped brush I made it in two strokes shown on the left in figure 233 —

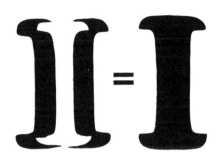

Fig. 233. Stem and block serifs for letter I made in two strokes.

•

a big saving in time and oddly, I believe a better letter with more natural reverse swelling to the stem. I am sure that other Chicago writers developed their own stroke patterns and sequences even though I do not recall discussing the matter with them. As apprentices we learned the general rule that letter strokes are written from top to bottom and from left to right. Additions and changes were made thereafter according to one's needs.

Figure 234 shows the strokes and sequences I used for making *Cooper Black* letters R and O. From these one can deduce most of the sequences to be followed for the remainder of the alphabet. Note particularly how the writer moves from left to right in making letter parts, for example, making first the left outer curve, then the left inner, right inner and finally the right outer curve of letter O and, not as one would think, making first the outer curves of O before finishing with the inner.[30] As in the letter H (Cf. figs. 230 and **231,**) one does not allow a kinesthetic trace to pass over a previously made, wet stroke.

Permanent signs in Rome were in stone, wood, stucco, and bronze.

Fig. 234. Lettering-writing stroke sequences for making Cooper Black letter I, R, and O, with the square edge, show-card brush.

•

For sign purposes, stone (in the Empire mostly marble) was as common as bronze and wood were scarce. It would appear then that there were many Roman makers of permanent signs who worked mostly in stone— enough to justify the assumption that there were technical constants, craft practices and similar ways of handling tools in that sign making trade.

In ancient Rome there was no fashion in alphabets such as we have today, nor did the Romans have to contend with the bewildering multiplicity of caps, lower-case, italic, decorative initials, scripts, Black letters, sans-serif, etc. In the Imperium there was one, fixed majuscular alphabet that so resisted change and idiosyncratic tamperings for almost two centuries, that today, only the knowledgeable paleographer can attribute, say, the better Hadrianic and Augustan letter shapes.

278

Let us make another comparison between Rome and Chicago. If we contrast the great number of non-professional, informal writers—lawyers, clerks, teachers, students, business people, housewives, etc., in Chicago with the number of sign writers the number of sign writers would be quite small. But if one were to make a like census apportion in Trajan's Rome he would find the proportion of sign makers to other letter users would be much larger,[31] and that these sign makers would be working in the sign industry's chief work—inscription writing and cutting marble.

The square-shaped brush was common to both Chicago and Rome. While we have no actual archeologic remains of such brushes, the letters written by Romans demonstrate beyond any doubt their existence. Certainly we know that brushes were in use several thousand years before the Imperium, For example, the Egyptians used brushes made of fibrous woods, rushes, reeds, grasses bound together much like today's camel hair quills used by sign painters, and that the Latin word for brush *penicillum,* meant "little tail" since brushes were made of ox hair, horse hair, etc.

With letter shapes in Rome firmly fixed by the reed it would then be a simple and logical step to the square-edged brush for larger, inscription writing. After all, the Romans, having reduced Egypt to a province, had ample opportunity to adopt the chisel-shaped writing tool used by the Egyptians for many centuries. A glance at the Hadrianic inscription from Africa (Fig. 111), the inscriptions from Narbonne, Pompeii, Rome, etc., shown in figures 104 through 124, makes it hazardous for anyone to deny that these were written with anything other than a square-edged, chisel-shaped brush.

So we can assign, as constants, linking 20th century Chicago sign-writing to the Imperial sign writing 1) the square, chisel-shaped brush, and 2) speed, from which would follow such corollaries as stroke-sequences, -directions, cant changes, and brush manipulation. The fact of speed is made clear from the economy of chisel cutting—shallow V-cuts in which less stone is cut away, hence greater production of inscriptions—and from the fact that the inscription layout was written directly

279

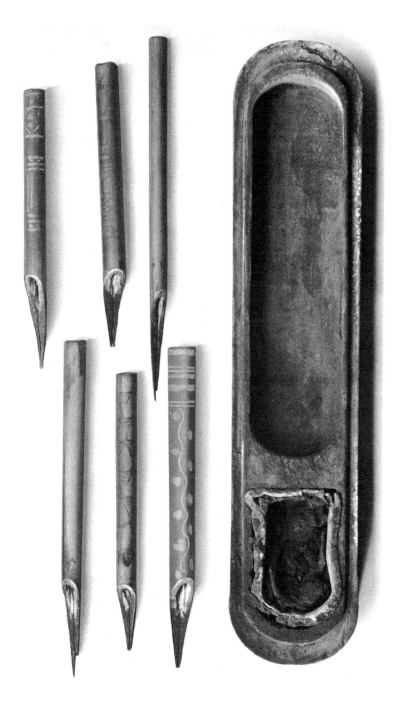

Fig. 235. Egyptian reeds from the Roman Period, first century B.C. British Museum.

and not lettered tediously by out-lining, patterns, or double-lined methods. The fact of the brush and its special handling, without exception, is evident from every part of every letter and mark in the better Imperial signs.

Our comparisons show that the Chicago writers of the early 20th century, totally unaware of it, had a great deal in common with Imperial Roman inscription makers and are the direct heirs of the Roman, brush-writing tradition; that both are craft brothers engaged in the trade of sign writing, and had, by some miracle, a "brother" from one age been reincarnated into the other, he would have been able to take his place as a journeyman worker in the local sign-writing shop, whether in Trajan's Rome or Capone's Chicago.

I do not imply that Trajan letters were written in Chicago or vice versa, but the basic brush usage was the same in both. Had a master professional writer of Chicago wished he could have written Imperial inscriptions; similarly, the Trajan writing master could easily have adjusted to Marshall Field's brush writing demands in the 1920's.

Years ago in a discussion with Langdon Warner regarding calligraphy and slate chiselling during the Han Dynasties (206 B.C.-200 A.D.) in China, I outlined the main points of the Rome-Chicago kinship-theory. At the time I was fascinated with the possibility of some sort of cultural or craft tie between the contemporaneous Imperial inscription craft and Han Dynasty tomb carvings, notably carvings in micaceous schist (a slatelike stone) from North China, of which he had many fine rubbings (now preserved in the Fogg Museum archives at Harvard.) I hoped that this culture, existing side by side with the Imperium, would yield some corroboration for my belief that, to the Roman scribe and letter-cutter, writing was the important item in monumental inscriptions.

Warner was deeply interested, and said that it was known that in the second and third century B.C. Rome traded for silk and other wares with Serica (China) and that along with the economic went a certain amount of cultural interchange. Whether such an exchange touched on calligraphy no one could as yet affirm or deny. But it seemed to him far

281

more probable that the following of like procedure, even in utterly different cultures such as Old China, ancient Rome and our Chicago, would result in like effects, and that of these likenesses the most striking to him was the primacy of brush writing over all other graphic expressions.

36

Summary

Listing the chief points in this study of the brush and serif we find that Imperial inscriptions were:

1- first brush written
2- including their serifs
3- and characteristic letter parts,
4- then V-cut in stone.
5- The V-cut was painted with red-orange
6- to restore the original writing of the inscription.
7- Written letters existed before chiselled shapes,
8- and writing was the important item
9- and not chiselling the writing.
10- Chiselling is a means not an end,
11- and had nothing to do with serif origin,
12- nor with the formation of letter shapes,
13- nor did chiselling aid legibility.
14- The chiselled V-cut helped to preserve the writing
15- by shielding the letters below the stone surface
   away from weathering agencies.
16- Letters were thought of as linear, 2-dimensional
   shapes
17- hence V-cuts were shallow
18- with no concern for shadows.
19- In modern times emphasis on shadows
20- led to false theories of letter-proportions and
   -formation.

21- The chisel's sole contribution is a small-scale striation in the V-cut.

22- Any shape written by the brush can be cut in stone,

23- and it is no more difficult to chisel curved than straight letter parts.

24- The lapidary letter is not the parent of Roman and western calligraphy.

25- Rome's singular invention was shaded writing.

26- with 25-30 degrees cant

27- which gave a thick-and-thin, 2 : 1 proportion characteristic of roman letters.

28- The first Latin scripts were formal,

29- followed by semi-formal and informal scripts when writers became familiar with the formal alphabet.

30- The script known by all Roman readers was the pattern for the Latin librarial bookhand

31- which in turn was the model for Monumental letters, Rustic, and Square Capitals.

32- Formal script favors the eye that reads and

33- informal the hand that writes letters.

34- The importance of kinesthesis in writing has been overlooked as well as

35- its connection with the 'minusculizing tendency.'

36- Inscription writers were probably professional scribes, that is, *librarii* or book publishers ('printers').

37- The square-edged brush, sophisticated child of the reed, differs from all other writing tools.

38- It added new dimension to letter making.

39- Unlike the reed it is able to change cant much more easily while writing letter parts.

40- The brush begins and ends every stroke by coursing along its thin edge ('edge-in' and 'edge-out')

41- and this 'edging' stroke is the real origin of the serif

2- and of the fillet which connects the arm (or stem)
   with the serif.
43- The broad, ox-bow, bracketed serif did not
    originate in Greece
44- rather it is a unique Roman contribution to
    western letters.
45- In the Imperium Roman inscription makers were
    professional sign writers.
46- Rome's inscription making likened to Chicago's
    sign-writing craft of the early 20th century
47- by reason of speed and brush handling common
    to both.

•

Much remains to be learnt about letters. The views advanced here
cannot be final. There are certainly gaps to be found in it, and perhaps
even some errors. In printing it I have the hope that my brother calligraphers will find here a footing for theory, discussion, and practice more
rockfast and sure than the sands we have inherited from the Renaissance.

37

1. Compare sepulchral inscriptions from Praeneste dating from 250-215 B.C. *Corpus Inscriptionum Latinarum* (C.I.L.), (Berlin: Royal Prussian Academy, 1863-1916), vol. XIV, nos. 3052, 3077, 3079, 3188.

2. Could this be Demetrius, Martial's "trusted copyist," whose "calligraphy was a treasure to the Caesars?" ("illa manus . . . nota Caesaribus . . .") *Epig.* 101, Bk. 1.

3. Bronze sculpture, since the Renaissance, has been similarly influenced, that is, left ungilded. In fact, it is quite common to patinate, "age," and "antique" bronze artificially today. Very rarely is bronze gilded — the common practice of old.

4. In the Renaissance, letters acquired pictorial, '3-dimensional' solidity particularly in 'memento mori,' block books, historiated initials, etc.

5. The 3-D aberration, as far as I know, began in the historiated initials of the late medieval and early Renaissance illuminated books.

6. For example, Greek Uncials developed out of formal, Greek bookhand in the third century B.C.

7. Emil Hübner, *Exemplae Scripturae Epigraphicae Latinae a Caesaris Dictatoris morte ad Aetatem Justiniani* (Berlin: G. Reimerum, 1885), xxxiii, nos. 1146-52.

8.   E. A. Lowe, "Handwriting," from *The Legacy of the Middle Ages,* edited by G. C. Crump and E. F. Jacob (Oxford: Clarendon Press, 1926), p. 206.

9.   Petronius' phrase in *Satyricon,,* 29, 'Beware of the dog' written on the entrance wall of Trimalchio's house may be of help if one interprets the use of the singular number *(littera quadrata)* in the phrase to mean a large monumental script as made by the quadrator, otherwise, the term is ambiguous.

   A later phrase in *Satyricon* 58, *Non didici geometrias, critica et alogas maenias, sed lapidarias litteras scio.* "I never learned geometry, criticism, or such nonsense, but I know how to read words carved in stone . . ." is more meaningful.

10.   This motion is prevalent today, e.g., David Diringer's excellent book, *The Alphabet* (New York: Philosophical Library, 1948), p. 541, says: ". . . the 'monumental' script; . . . was called 'square,' because of its rectilinear formation and the mainly rectangular junctions of the strokes; . ." but one suspects that Dr. Diringer, a non-calligrapher, was only quoting a well-known calligrapher-author.

11.   The term "Square Capitals" is now firmly established and I am not suggesting that we should find a substitute for it. But we should, I think, be aware of its illegitimate ancestry. The term *Capitale Elegante* (Elegant or Refined Capitals) used by Professor Giulio Battelli of the Pontifical Institute of Paleography seems more apt.

12.   ". . — the square capitals . . . are merely a pen-drawn variety of lapidary capitals . . ." Frederic W. Goudy, *The Alphabet,"* p. 36.

13.   And thus showing its majuscule-to-minuscule devolution, provided, of course, the F is written in the correct stroke sequence.

14. Edward Maunde Thompson, *An Introduction to Greek and Latin Palaeography* (Oxford: Clarendon Press, 1912), p. 313.

---

15. St. Paul (*Ad Tim. II*, 4, 13) reminds Timothy to bring the books, especially the parchment ones, and Martial mentions the works of Homer, Virgil, and other authors preserved on parchment.

---

16. The presence in the third century B.C. of rudimentary serifs in inscriptions from Praeneste hints at the use of a square-edged brush or frayed reed which produced these terminals. In turn these Praenestine serifs suggest that shaded writing may have had its beginnings even earlier, in the second half of the third century B.C.

---

17. That is, formal and semi-formal inscriptions written in *wax-coated* bronze tablets prior to acid etching.

---

18. Though some letters were cut in stone with chisels (hard tools) such letters are *first* formally conceived and made by *soft* writing tools.

---

19. In the development and lineage theory for the early Roman alphabet illustrated in figure 161, there was no need to show letter development and branching after the pre-Caroline scripts. There is no disagreement among scholars as to placement and filiation of subsequent scripts such as Gothic, Batarde, Papal Chancery, Caroline, etc. Some readers may resent this truncation after pre-Caroline. There is no denying that Roman letter origins and branchings from antiquity to our times are of general interest to students and calligraphers and this more so if a new viewpoint is projected. Accordingly I have expanded figure 161 into a full-sized chart, along with explanatory notes, showing alphabetic expression for western letters from the first archaic Latin capitals down to contemporary Spencerian scrawling. While they

288

last, readers may obtain this colored chart, titled *A Theory of Development and Lineage for the Roman Alphabet,* from the Mohawk Paper Mills, Cohoes, N. Y., 12047.

20. *Acta Diurna,* published daily in Rome by government authority during the late Republic and under the Empire (Tacitus, *Annales,* iii, 3; xiii, 31; xvi, 22; Petronius, Cap. 53; Cicero, *Ad Fam.,* ii, 15; viii, 1; xiii, 8). After the acts were written up they were officially exposed to the public where they could be read by the people and copied by scribes — especially for the wealthy (some of whom had their own private 'Pony Express') in Rome and the provinces.

21. Some teachers, e.g., use rhythmic, musical accompaniments to writing exercises, under the erroneous notion that there is a tempo-equality and interval time-spacing in shaping letters.

22. Some sign men call this "knife-in" and "knife-out."

23. A possible exception may be "cupping" of head and foot-serifs in type faces. It is doubtful though that the cupped serif is derived from or suggested by its reverse shape, the dent of inscription letters. Cupping appears to be a type designer's contribution to offset the vertical weight of main stems which tend to make serifs appear convex rather than straight across.

24. The calligrapher who wrote the Trajan Inscription apparently defended and emphasized the baseline. With the exception of Q's tail, most letters sit firmly *on the baseline.* Few cross it.

25. Edward Johnston and A.E.R. Gill, *Manuscript and Inscription Letters for Schools and Classes and for the Use of Craftsmen* (London: Isaac Pitman, Ltd. 1922). Plate 16.

26. Practically all lettering and calligraphy manuals continue teaching the wrong method. I do not know of a single engineering, architectural, or mechanical drawing text that teaches the correct stroke sequence and direction for making letters.

27. Even with this advantage, on becoming a union, card-carrying "professional" sign writer, I lost my first two jobs because I was not "fast enough." I held my first job for half a day and the second two days.

28. Named after Oswald Cooper, the brilliant and gifted Chicago calligrapher-typographer whose letter-face was quickly picked up by the show-card writers and theater-lobby, poster artists in the 20's.

29. Inasmuch as there is a fixed, economical pattern of stroke sequences and directions for making such letters one could call this a *writing-lettering* method.

30. This method (writing-lettering) lies between writing and lettering for, according to our definition, essential letter parts are made in more than one stroke, yet, unlike lettering, these strokes are made in a regularly followed sequence, direction and number as in writing.

31. Nor ought we to overlook, for example, that slaves (purposely kept illiterate) once outnumbered freemen at least twenty to one, and that education (hence calligraphy) was specifically reserved for a small minority.

Index

A

A, letter, 8, 29, 34, 65, 66, 77, 143, 197, 198, 199, 203, 204, 205, 206, 207, 210, 221, 222, 224, 225, 228, 229, 267.
Abacus, 63
Abbreviations, 41
Abecedarium of Albegna, Marsilian, 151, 152, 153
Accidentals, 12, 110
Aberration, 3-D, 286
Acta Diurna, 289
Accounts, 98
Acid scrubbing, 67
Action of the brush, 172
Actuarial letters, 159
Advanced amateurs, 81
Advertising alphabets, 14
Advertisements in Rome, 158, 159
Aeolic-Chalcidian Greeks, 98
Age of Specialization, 268
Ahenobarbus, 271
Alphabet, first age of an, 140; of 24 letters, 112; Roman Forum inscription, 139; stones, 79, 80, 217
Alphabetic expressions in early Rome and after, 157; lineage, 151; roots before the Imperium, 151
Amateur brush writers, 169; scribes, 148, 149
American Academy of Arts, Rome, 122, 125
American School for Classical Studies, Athens, 51
Amphora di Formello, Chigi, 152
Anatomical proportions, 112
Ancient letter cutters fast, 117; records, 108; sign writers, 116; painted Roman inscriptions, 82

Angled bottoms of letters, 206; ends, 30; tops, 206, 207
Anglo-Saxon, 157
Angular curves, 36
Angular junctures, 18, 35, 76
Angular letter parts, 95
Anti-Gothic reaction, 61
Apex, 77
Aphrodite, 159
"Aphrodite of Cnidus", 60
Arch of Septimius Severus, 136
Archaic capitals, 150, 153, 157; Latin, 138, 289
Architectural letters, 77, 270; manuals, 77
Arm endings, 203, 204; serifs, 49, 86, 113, 133, 175, 178, 179, 180, 195, 196
Arm of T, 195
Arms, 16, 17, 32, 34, 35, 50, 87, 89, 177, 178, 184, 187; arms, rounded, 202
Arm serif determines serif-scale, 179
"Arts and Crafts" movement, 61, 62
Artistic unity, 61
Arundo Donas, 98
Ascenders, 164
Assyrian, 37, 65
Athens National Epigraphic Museum, 37, 38, 39
Attributes of brush and reed, 182
Auditory cliches, 102
Auditory expectancy, 102
Augustus, Forum of, 123
Augustan inscription, 117, 161; interpoints, 189; letters, 199, 207, 279
Authors dismissing the brush, 170, 171
"Automatic pilot", 142

Y

Z

39

Acknowledgments

thank those who read and criticized the manuscript and those who allowed me to make photographs, rubbings, and squeezes of material in the monuments and museums under their directtion: Gabriella Begni, National Museum of Villa Giulia, Rome; Giacomo Caputo, Superintendent of Etruscan Antiquities, National Archeological Museum, Florence; Norman Cram, of R. R. Donnelley & Sons, Chicago; I. E. S. Edwards, Keeper, Dept. of Egyptian Antiquities, British Museum, London; Alfonso de Franciscis, National Museum of Antiquities, Naples; Italo Foldi, Luigi Pigorini Museum of Ethnography and Prehistory, Rome; Guglielmo Gatti, Director of Monuments and Excavations of Rome; Professor Dr. A. Greifenhagen, Director, National Museum, Dept. of Greek and Roman Antiquities, Berlin; Philip Hofer, Director, Houghton Library, Harvard University; J. J. Johns, Institute for Advanced Study, Princeton; Norbert Kunisch, Dept. of Greek and Roman Antiquities, National Museum, Berlin; Wolfgang Muller, Director, Egyptian Antiquities, National Museum, East Berlin, (DDR); Nina del Museos, National Epigraphic Museum, Athens; Lloyd Reynolds, Reed College, Portland, Oregon; Francesco Roncalli, Conte di Montorio, Vatican Lapidary Galleries, Vatican City; the late Langdon Warner, Chairman, Dept. of Far Eastern Art, Fogg Museum, Cambridge.

I owe special thanks to the President and Administrative Council of St. Ambrose College for a partial grant towards the publication of this volume. December 7, 1967.

40

Colophon

Fr. Catich clarified his procedure, "The typeface is 12 pt. Linotype Baskerville. The chapter-heading and title-page alphabets are of my design as are the typographic flourishes, initials and end papers."

This printing is from the same film which Fr. Catich used. It is printed on acid-free paper chosen to match closely the original printing.

abcdefghijklmnopqrstuvwxyz

ABCDEFGHIJKLMNOPQRSTUVWXYZ

&

ABCDEFGHIJKLMNOPQRSTUVWXYZ

$123456789 $1234567890

abcdefghijklmnopqrstuvwxyz

ABCDEFGHIJKLMNOPQRSTUVWXYZ

&

$1234567890

309

&

ABCDEFGHIJKLMN
OPQRSTUVWXYZ
&
abcdefghijklmnopqrst
uvwxyzawtti
234567890?
ffi

ABCDEFGHIJKLMN
OPQRSTUVWXYZ